D1093492

PINOCHLE

HOW TO PLAY · HOW TO WIN

PINOCHLE

HOW TO PLAY · HOW TO WIN

By Walter Gibson

CASTLE BOOKS

Distributed by
BOOK SALES, INC.
110 Enterprise Avenue
Secaucus, N.J. 07094

Part 1

Introduction to Pinochle

Part 2

Types of Games

Part I Introduction to Pinochle

RULES

AND

PROCEDURES

This game, which is played in varied form, utilizes a special pack of 48 cards, from Ace down to Nine in each suit, with each duplicated. The Ten ranks next to the Ace in value, so the cards run downward — A, A, 10, 10, K, K, Q, Q, J, J, 9, 9.

In play, there is always a trump, so a card of that suit takes a trick when played on leads from other suits. Otherwise, the card of highest value in the lead suit takes the trick. If two identical cards are played on one trick as the **A ♦** and the **A ♦**, the one played first wins.

From 12 to 16 cards are dealt to each player — according to the type of game — and from these, a player can form combinations known as *melds* which he shows to the other players and by such declaration gains points toward his score.

These melds fall into the following categories:

A	Trump Sequence: A,10,K,Q,J	*150 points*
	Royal Marriage: K and Q of trumps	*40 points*
	Plain Marriage: K and Q of any suit	*20 points*
B	Pinochle: formed by **J♦** and **Q♠**	*40 points*
	Double Pinochle: **J♦,J♦,Q♠, Q♠**	*80 points*
C	Four Aces in different suits	*100 points*
	Four Kings in different suits	*80 points*
	Four Queens in different suits	*60 points*
	Four Jacks in different suits	*40 points*
D	Nine of trump, called *Dix* or *Deece*	*10 points*

A card can be used only once in a meld of its own type; but it can be used in a meld of another type. The following is an example;

A player forms a trump sequence ♠: A, 10, K, Q, J. He cannot add the other **K♠** to the **Q♠** in the sequence to form a Royal Marriage as both melds are *Type A*.

However, he could add the **J♦** to the **Q♠** and call it a Pinochle, which is *Type B*. He could add the **Q♦, Q♥, Q♣** to the **Q♠** to form Four Queens, which belong in *Type C*.

Similarly, he could add the **K♣** to the **Q♣** to form a Plain Marriage, since the **Q♣** is in a *Type C* meld and the new marriage would be *Type A*.

Since the **J♦**, above, is so far only in *Type B*, and the **J♠** only in *Type A*, the **J♣** and **J♥** could be added to them to form Four Jacks, which is *Type C*.

But he could not add a second **Q♠** to the present **J♦**, as it already forms a Pinochle, *Type B*, with a **Q♠**, or he would be using the **J**♦ twice in a meld of the same type.

There is also a special meld known as a Round House or Round Trip that applies in certain games. It is composed of four Kings and four Queens, one of each suit, which also form a Royal Marriage and three Plain Marriages, giving the player 240 points for the meld.

After declaring melds, the same cards are used in play, along with any that were not melded. A player is credited with points for winning specific cards, according to one of the following schedules, each of which totals 240 points.

Original		*Simplified*		*Popular*	
Each Ace	*11*	Each Ace	*10*	Each Ace	*10*
Each Ten	*10*	Each Ten	*10*	Each Ten	*10*
Each King	*4*	Each King	*10*	Each King	*5*
Each Queen	*3*	Last Trick	*10*	Each Queen	*5*
Each Jack	*2*			Last Trick	*10*
Last Trick	*10*				

Procedure varies with various forms of Pinochle, so each will be treated individually in the chapters that follow.

Part II Types of Games

I

THREE-HANDED PINOCHLE

This is the simplest form of Pinochle and therefore is the best introduction to the game, as it is easy to follow and an excellent game in its own right. From it have stemmed the more popular game of *Auction Pinochle* and still more modern types of partnership play, which will be described in due course, but since all follow the basic pattern of the three-handed game, you have a lot to gain and nothing to lose by considering it as a starter.

In Three-Handed Pinochle; the players cut the shuffled pack and the one drawing the highest card becomes the first dealer; in case of a tie, which frequently occurs, the players involved cut the cards again. The dealer then shuffles the pack, which is cut by the player on his right and sixteen cards are dealt by fours to each player. The dealer, however, turns up the final card of his hand and places it to one side to designate the trump suit for that deal.

If the turned-up card is the Dix, or Nine of Trumps, the dealer melds a preliminary 10 points for himself and takes the Dix into his hand. The player holding the other Dix also shows it and melds 10 points. If any other trump is turned up, the player to the dealer's left can pick it up by discarding a Dix to replace it, melding 10 points in the process. That is, provided he has a Dix; if not, the privilege goes to the next player. Sometimes, the dealer holds both Nines of Trumps, so he simply shows them, melding 10 for each Dix, and automatically taking the turned-up trump card for himself, in order to complete his hand. But if one of the other players picked up the turned-up trump, the dealer is forced to take up the discarded Dix.

Each player then makes regular melds, forming all the allowable combinations that he can by laying the necessary cards face up in front of him. These are duly recorded on a score sheet and the players take their melds back into their hands, ready for the play that follows.

The play should properly begin with the player at the dealer's left, as with most games in which a trump is turned up. If preferred, it can start with the dealer, but this should be settled by agreement beforehand. Actually, it makes very little difference, but since the original practice was to open at the dealer's left, that rule will be followed in the present discussion.

Whatever card the first player leads, the next player must follow suit, playing a Heart on a Heart, a Club on a Club, and so on, with the highest card taking the trick. If unable to follow suit, a player must play a trump if he has one and the trump takes the trick, unless overtrumped by the next player. If unable to follow suit or trump, a player must throw on a card from another suit, which has no *taking* power.

However, whenever a trump is led, the next player must play a higher trump if he has one, and the next player must do the same, if he can. This is called *heading the trick* and is an important part of Pinochle play, as it enables a player to use low trumps to force out high trumps more rapidly. This does not apply when the lead of an ordinary suit is trumped by the second player. The third player, if also out of the suit led, does not have to overtrump the second player, although he can do so if he wants.

Note: The rule of *heading the trick* once applied to ordinary suits as well as trump, but is not used in the modern forms of Pinochle. Hence, although the standard three-handed game dates back to when the rule was in vogue, it has been eliminated from this game as well, unless players agree to include it, which they seldom, if ever, do. But the rule is each successive player must try to head a trick when a trump is led, is one that is universally accepted.

Therefore, the player who takes a trick leads to the next trick and this continues until the hand has been played. Each player looks through the tricks that he has taken and totals the number of points that he has, adding them to his meld for that deal, but with this important proviso: If a player fails to take a trick, he loses his meld for that deal and it is erased from his running score. Taking one lone trick is sufficient to save his meld, whether or not that trick contains a *counter* according to whichever schedule is used.

The cards are then gathered and the deal moves to the player on the left. This continues, deal by deal, turning up a new trump with each deal, each player adding more scores to his column as the game continues. The game is 1,000 points and by the original rule, a player reaching that total declares *out* and the game ends; SUBJECT TO THE FOLLOWING FACTORS:

If a player's meld brings his score to 1,000 or higher, he must take a trick before declaring *out,* since otherwise, his meld does not count. Hence, if two — or even three — players go beyond the 1,000 mark with a meld, the first to take a trick automatically becomes the winner.

If a player takes sufficient counters during the course of play to reach 1,000 or beyond, he stops after taking the trick that puts him out, thanks to the counter or counters it contains, and this is verified to prove his claim. Thus it is possible that Player X, with a score of 940 might meld 80, giving him a total of 1020, while Player Y, with a score of 840, might meld 120, giving him only 960. But if "Y" could take two tricks, with a total of 40, before "X" could take any, "Y" would hit the 1,000 mark and win, since the meld made by "X" would be canceled due to his failure to take a trick.

By this ruling, ties are impossible, because the *trick taker* is a sure winner, unless he pulls a "boo-boo" and declares *out* when he is still *in*. Actually, this should never happen, because when the game is that close, each player should be counting every point that he takes in with each trick. There is no case on record where such a stupid mistake was ever made, so the simple solution is, that if it ever should happen, the other players should condone it as a mental lapse on the part of the player who unwittingly boo-booed it.

NOW FOR THE OTHER WAY OF DETERMINING THE WINNER:

All hands are played out to the finish, with scores totalled accordingly. If more than one player has reached the 1,000 mark, the game continues, with 1,250 as the goal. If two players pass that mark in the same deal, the goal is upped another 250, making it 1,500; and so on, until one player emerges as the winner. This raises the question: What about the third player? If he failed to reach the 1,000 mark along with the other two, what then?

The best answer is, to have him stay in the game and if he can forge ahead and reach the 1,250 mark before the others, more power to him. Giving the low man a *free ride* adds interest to the game whenever a tight finish looms in the offing. However:

There is still a simpler way of deciding on a winner. That is to count all the points after the final hand and award the game to the player with the highest score above 1,000. If "X" finishes with 1,060, he wins over "Y" with 1,040, or "Z" with 1,010. If the two highest have identical scores of 1,050, another hand is played by all three on the same *high to win* basis.

When the game is played for ships or stakes, the winner collects from each of his rivals, regardless of the margin of victory. In match play, the first player to win a stipulated number of games, say three, wins the match.

Playing the Hands

At the outset, each player in a game of Three-Handed Pinochle is strictly on his own and this pattern usually continues throughout. So the best way to study the fine points is by means of a sample deal, involving three players: Andy, Brad and Chet. It is Chet's deal and the hands run as follows:

Andy:	♣: 10,10,K,Q,J	♦: A,10,K,9,9
	♠: K,K,9	♥: K,J,9
Brad:	♣: A,Q,9*(K)	♦: A,10,Q
	♠: A,10,10,Q,J,9	♥: A,10,10,Q

Chet:	♣: A,J,9,(9)	♦: K,Q,J,J
	♠: A,Q,J	♥: A,K,Q,J,9
	Turned-up as Trump:	**K♣**

*With Clubs as Trump, Brad shows the Dix (**9♣**) and melds 10 points, discarding the **9♣** and taking up the **K♣** (indicated in parentheses).

Chet also shows a Dix and melds 10 and has to take up the Dix that Brad discarded (indicated in parentheses), but it counts nothing.

The players then meld as follows:

Andy:	Four Kings (**K♣,K♠,K♦,K♥**)	80
	Royal Marriage (**K♣,Q♣**)	40
	Total	120
Brad:	Four Aces (**A♣,A♠,A♦,A♥**)	100
	Four Queens (**Q♣,Q♠,Q♦,Q♥**)	60
	Royal Marriage (**K♣,Q♣**)	40
	Plus Dix (**9♣**) already melded	10
	Total	210
Chet:	Pinochle (**J♦** & **Q♠**)	40
	Four Jacks (**J♦,J♠,J♥,J♣**)	40
	Two Marriages (**K♦,Q♦** & **K♥,Q♥**)	40
	Plus Dix (**9♣**) already shown	10
	Total	130

The melds are entered conditionally upon the score sheet and each player takes his melded cards back in his hand, after carefully noting what the others have melded, which is an important thing in Pinochle. Going by the rule that play starts with the player on the dealer's left, Andy leads to the first trick.

Here, the **A♦** would be a fairly obvious lead on Andy's part, since each of the other players melded Diamonds, so he is sure to win the trick. But it may serve him better, later on, so he decides to force out trumps instead, hoping to make his two Tens good:

1st Trick:
Andy: **J♣** Brad: **A♣** Chet: **9♣** Brad Wins
2nd Trick:
Brad: **A♦** Chet: **J♦** Andy: **9♦** Brad Wins
3rd Trick:
Brad: **A♠** Chet: **J♠** Andy: **9♠** Brad Wins
4th Trick:
Brad: **A♥** Chet: **9♥** Andy: **9♥** Brad Wins

Brad has cashed his Aces and now wants to get rid of his two Diamonds, on the chance of trumping that suit later.

5th Trick:
Brad: **Q♦** Chet: **J♦** Andy: **K♦** Andy Wins
6th Trick:
Andy: **Q♣** Brad: **K♣** Chet: **A♣** Chet Wins
7th Trick:
Chet: **A♠** Andy: **K♠** Brad: **9♠** Chet Wins
8th Trick:
Chet: **A♥** Andy: **J♥** Brad: **Q♥** Chet Wins

Chet has copied Brad's policy of using his Aces and now gets rid of his last Spade, hoping to trump that suit later.

9th Trick:
Chet: **Q♠** Andy: **K♠** Brad: **10♠** Brad Wins
10th Trick:
Brad: **10♦** Chet: **Q♦** Andy: **A♦** Andy Wins
11th Trick:
Andy: **10♣** Brad: **Q♣** Chet: **9♣** Andy Wins
12th Trick:
Andy: **10♣** Brad: **J♠** Chet: **J♣** Andy Wins

Neat work here. Brad, taking the 9th trick with the **10♠** was doubly smart. Suspecting that Chet was out of Spades, he held back his other **10♠** and led his **10♦**, hoping the other players would think he had more. But Andy, winning the 10th trick with the **A♦**, guessed Brad's ruse and held back his **10♦**. Figuring that *both* Chet and Andy still held at least one trump in hand, Andy led a **10♣** to the 11th trick and another **10♣** to the 12th, forcing out all the trumps. Andy then takes over with:

13th Trick:
Andy: **10♦** Brad: **Q♠** Chet: **K♦** Andy Wins
14th Trick:
Andy: **9♦** Brad: **10♥** Chet: **J♥** Andy Wins
15th Trick:
Andy: **K♥** Brad: **10♥** Chet: **Q♥** Brad Wins
16th Trick:
Brad: **10♠** Chet: **K♥** Andy: **K♣** Andy Wins

Note how Andy cleaned the Diamonds on the 13th trick and made good with the **9♦** on the 14th. He could have led the **K♣** to the 15th trick, winning it with ease; but he might then have lost the **K♥** on the 16th trick. So he threw away the **K♥** on the 15th; and why? Because the 16th trick was the *Last Trick* which counts 10 points in its own right; and Andy wanted those 10 points. That's how closely you figure it in Pinochle, which is why so many people think that Pinochle is a great game.

Going through the tricks taken by each player, the counters are checked and evaluated, according to the particular schedule agreed upon. In this case, they will be listed by all three counts, Original, Simplified and Popular, by way of comparison, as follows:

Andy's Tricks

	As	10s	Ks	Qs	Js
No. of Counters	1	6	4	4	4
Original	11	60	16	12	8
Simplified	10	60	40	—	—
Popular	10	60	20	20	—

Last Trick 10

Brad's Tricks

	As	10s	Ks	Qs	Js
No. of Counters	4	2	2	2	3
Original	44	20	8	6	6
Simplified	40	20	20	—	—
Popular	40	20	10	10	—

Chet's Tricks

	As	10s	Ks	Qs	Js
No. of Counters	3	0	2	2	1
Original	33	0	8	6	2
Simplified	30	0	20	—	—
Popular	30	0	10	10	—

Total Counts

	Original	Simplified	Popular
Andy's Points:	127	120	120
Brad's Points:	84	80	80
Chet's Points:	79	50	50

Note that the Original count varied only slightly from the Simplified and Popular, which came out exactly the same in each case. This is somewhat unusual, as there is apt to be a variance of 5 to 10 points, though seldom much more. This indicates that the type of *count* matters very little, though many Pinochle players lay great stress on this factor. For convenience in scoring, the Simplified Count (A = 10, 10 =

10, K = 10) is best, as it produces totals in terms of tens, so it will be used in this case.

At the end of the deal just described, the score sheet stands:

ANDY		BRAD		CHET	
Dix	10		—	Dix	10
Meld	120	Meld	200	Meld	120
Count	120	Count	80	Count	50
Totals	250		280		180

So far, the game is reasonably close, as one good meld in the next hand — such as a Sequence (150) or Four Aces (100) — will enable Chet to close the margin between himself and the leader, Brad. So each player operates strictly on his own for the next few hands, at least; but if one player, such as Brad, should be far ahead when he nears the 1,000 mark, the other two, Andy and Chet, may find it necessary to resort to *cut-throat* tactics.

Say that Brad has a score of 780 at the end of the third deal, with Andy only 670 and Chet 650. On the fourth deal, Brad makes a meld of 120 bringing him to 900, while Andy only melds 60 to reach 730, and Chet 50 to reach 700. It is obvious that if Brad takes 100 in counters, he will win the game. So during play, if Andy leads a winning Ace, Chet, instead of throwing out a worthless Nine, plays a high counter like a Ten, letting Andy take it, rather than run the risk of having Brad gather it in later.

As play progresses, Brad may try to force out trumps by leading the last card of an odd suit, hoping that both Chet and Andy will waste trumps on it. But it happens that by then, Andy is out of trumps. So when Chet trumps Brad's lead, Andy, instead of throwing a Nine from a side suit, tosses out a Ten or even an Ace from a suit that Andy trumped earlier. This gives Chet a valuable counter that might otherwise go to Brad.

As a result, Brad is stopped well short of the 1,000 mark and another hand is in order, thanks to Andy and Chet tossing counters each other's way. True, the score might stand with Brad 960, Andy 830 and Chet 790, which means that Brad is still well ahead. But with a fifth deal coming up, a meld of 100 or more by either would give Brad stiff competition if his own meld proved to be a dud. Of course, whichever made the big meld — Andy or Chet — the other would try to keep him from going out. In this game, two players only become pals long enough to serve THEIR individual needs.

Pinochle players often raise the question: What is the best hand a player can hold? Three-Handed Pinochle brings up some interesting slants regarding that question. There is a hand that rates nearly tops where the meld is concerned and therefore looks like one of the best, though it can turn out to be one of the worst. Here it is:

♦: K,K,Q,Q ♣: K,K,Q,Q, ♥: K,K,Q,Q, ♠: K,K,Q,Q

Eight Kings and Eight Queens make up a Double Roundhouse, which produces a meld of 480. But when you come to play it, your two opponents can gang up on you and take every trick, thus nullifying the meld and giving you a fat, round Zero (0) for that deal. That is, unless they should slip up in their play, which they shouldn't, because they see your entire hand when you make your meld and, therefore, each knows exactly what the other has. But the task can prove tough.

Each opponent has to zigzag his Aces and Tens back and forth, so they will take four tricks, two for each Ace, two for each Ten. If one uses an Ace to take a Ten, it may spoil the whole thing, as it can give you a chance to take a trick with one of your Kings. If one opponent has more trumps than the other, the one with the fewer trumps can lead a Jack or Nine from a side suit, thus forcing out the King of that suit, while the other opponent takes the trick with a low trump. But somewhere along the line, the boys must play out their trumps in order to throw off cards from side suits.

Don't worry yourself about it, because it is one of those things that may never happen; but it is worth careful consideration because similar situations may arise in actual play. It is almost impossible for two players to gang up on a third and prevent him from taking any tricks at all; but often, through keen cooperative effort, they can cut down the number of points that he takes in play until they amount to very little.

In contrast, however, there is the super-perfect hand that can only be found in Three-Handed Pinochle. Here it is:

♠:A,A,10,10,K,K,Q,Q,J,J ♥: A,A ♣: A,A ♦: A,A

There, you see sixteen cards in all, consisting of two Trump Sequences of 150 each, plus two sets of Four Aces, at 100 each, making a 500 meld. If you should have such a hand, you could lay it face up and collect another 250 for taking every trick, making a total of 750 points in all. Nobody could win a trick against that hand, and the nice thing is that there are some hands that are not quite that wonderful, but come close enough to it to be big winners in their own right.

There is just one flaw in the Three-Handed game. Every now and then, a player comes up with a hand that would be super-super-duper, except for one flaw. The trump that is turned up is not the trump that he needs. Imagine, having a Double Sequence in Spades, only to have the dealer turn up some other suit for trump, which he almost had to do, because there were so few Spades left—only two, to be exact. So there was only one answer. Let the player with the big, big, wonderfun hand state what the trump should be.

And so, Auction Pinochle was born.

II

AUCTION PINOCHLE

Fifteen cards are dealt to each of three players, usually by threes, with three dealt aside as a *widow,* all cards being face down. The players look at their hands and either pass or bid the number of points which each thinks he can make in meld and play.

The player at the dealer's left starts the bidding and once a player has passed, he cannot bid again. Bidders, however, can raise each other as often as they wish. Usually, a minimum bid of either 250 or 300 is required; if no one will go that high, the hands are thrown in and dealt by the next dealer. Often, players agree to make the bidding start automatically. The player at the dealer's left *must* bid a minimum of 300.

No suit is specified during the bidding, as the highest bidder is allowed to name it afterward. Often the size of the bid has to do with his choice of suit; still more often, the widow is the important factor, as it goes to the successful bidder.

Consider the following sample hand.

♦: A,A,10,K,K,J ♠: A,K,Q,J,9 ♥: A,K ♣: A,Q

With Diamonds as trump, the player has a meld of four Aces, 100, plus a Pinochle, 40, and a Plain Marriage in Spades, 20, for a total of 160. Its playing strength might warrant a bid of 300.

With Spades as trump, the King and Queen become a Royal Marriage, 40, and the **9♠** is worth 10 as Dix, raising the meld to 190, but lessening the playing strength. So the player would hold his choice of trump until picking up the widow.

Often, a player will bid beyond the hand's existing value in hope of *filling* some important meld from the widow. The hand shown has three such possibilities, each worth 100 points as minimum and thereby encouraging a player to go as high as 400 if necessary. The prospects are the **Q ♦** which would *fill* a trump sequence in Diamonds — A, 10, K, Q, J — adding 150 for a total meld of 310.

The **10♠** which would form a trump sequence in Spades, 150, but would eliminate the Royal Marriage, 40, thus adding 110 to the present 190, for a total meld of 300.

The **K♣** making Four Kings, 80, plus a Plain Marriage in Clubs, 20, coming to 100. This would bring the meld up to 260, with Diamonds trump; or 290, with Spades trump.

When a player wins a bid, the widow is turned face up so all can see it. The bidder then adds the three cards to his hand and makes his meld, laying the melded cards face up on the table. They must remain there while he discards three other cards, face down.

Assume that with the sample hand, the player bid 380 and that the widow contains these cards — **K♣**, **10♥**, **J♠**.

Because of the added playing strength from the **J♠**, he names Spades as trump and melds as follows.

A♦A♣A♥A♠	Four Aces	*100 points*
K♦K♣K♥K♠	Four Kings	*80 points*
Q♣ Q♠	Plain *and* Royal Marriages	*60 points*
J♦	Pinochle, **J♦** with **Q♠**	*40 points*
9♠	Dix, Nine of trumps	*10 points*

This gives him a meld of 290, while his hand still contains the following:

♦: A,10,K ♠: J,J ♥: 10

From these, he discards the **10♦**, **K♦** and **10♥**, retaining the Jacks of Spades as added trump cards. Note that he has *put away* three counters worth 30 by the simplified count, or 25 if the popular count is used. Discarded widow cards go with any tricks the player takes, so he already has a nice start toward the 90 points that he must make to meet his bid of 380. He then adds the melded cards to his hand so it stands as follows:

♠: A,K,Q,J,J,9 ♦: A,A,K,J ♣: A,K,Q ♥: A,K

Play proceeds by the bidder leading any card he wishes to; the other two players must follow suit if possible. If a plain suit is led, and a player is out of it, he *must* trump it if he can; otherwise, he may throw off from a plain suit.

Only on the lead of a trump must the two players each play a higher trump, if they can. When a plain suit is led, the next two players must follow suit, or trump. But, if the second player trumps, the third player need not trump higher than the second player. For example, the first player plays a card in a suit in which both other players are void. If the second one trumps with a K, the third player must also trump, but he need not go higher than K.

This if often helpful to the bidder as he can force out opposing trumps by leading extra cards from an odd suit. However, the other players have a certain advantage from seeing the bidder's meld, as it enables them to appraise his losing cards.

The purpose of the opponents is to prevent the bidder from making his necessary score. To do this, they combine their efforts by throwing *counters* on each other's tricks, a process popularly styled *smearing*. They also make any leads that they feel will discommode the bidder.

Players once were required to head every trick that they could; that is, play higher when possible, no matter what suit happened to be led. That rule is long obsolete and now applies only when trump is led, as already stated.

As in most games, the winner of each trick leads to the next, and this continues to the end of the hand. The bidder keeps his tricks in one pile, while the opponents combine theirs. The 10 points for taking the last trick may often spell the difference between a successful bid and a loss, particularly if other counters come with it.

Each hand is like a separate game and the simplest way of scoring is on a plus and minus basis, according to specified levels, using chips or marking down the score. See the following example.

A bid of	250 to 290	wins or loses	5 chips each
A bid of	300 to 340	wins or loses	10 chips each
A bid of	350 to 390	wins or loses	15 chips each
A bid of	400 to 440	wins or loses	20 chips each

This can continue with the 450 level calling for 25 chips, the 500 level for 30 chips, and so on; but in many games, boosts are faster at the higher levels.

Some jump it up to 25 at the 400 level; 35 at 450; 45 at 500. Another way is to add 5 chips for each possible bid above 400, so that 410 is 25, 420 is 30, 430 is 35, and so on.

Other players go on the basis of 250, 5 chips; 300, 10 chips; then, 350, 20 chips; 400, 30 chips; continuing thus, with a jump of 10 chips at each level. Steepest of all is the *double up* which goes: 250, 5; 300, 10; 350, 20; 400, 40; 450, 80; 500, 160. Many variations are possible; any may be used as agreed.

Often, a player may meld enough to win his bid then and there, or come so close that no play is necessary. In that case, he simply collects on his bid. Thus, if he bid 330, he would take 10 chips each from his two opponents, winning 20 in all, according to the simple form of payment.

If he has overbid his hand and sees that he cannot make his bid or that the risk is too great, the bidder can *go bate*, admitting that he has failed and is beaten. Going *double bate* is a term used when a bidder plays the hand and loses. He must pay double — having played and lost. When a player takes the widow and realizes he has overbid and can't make the hand, he simply concedes the loss of game by throwing in his cards, refusing to play because he doesn't want to pay double. In that case, he would give 10 chips to each of his two opponents, losing 20 in all. Often a bidder prefers this out.

If a hand is played and lost, the bidder must pay double. Thus, if he bid 330 and only made a 320 score, each of his two opponents would receive 20 chips, the bidder losing 40 in all. Usually, the opponents insist on playing a hand through if there is even the slightest chance of stopping the bidder; but quite often, a bidder will throw in a doubtful hand.

Spades Double and Hearts Triple

This is specially true when playing *Spades Double*. This is an almost universal rule in Auction Pinochle. By it, a bid in Spades means that all payments are doubled, win or lose. Thus a player bidding 330 and declaring Spades trump would win 20 chips from each opponent, or 40 in all.

However, if he simply *concedes* and throws in his hand without naming trump, his loss would only be 10 to each opponent or 20 chips in all. As a result, it is often good policy to bid high on a hand that has possibilities in Spades, banking on improvement from the widow.

If a bidder plays and loses after bidding Spades, he pays double for losing, at the double rate for Spades, or 40 chips to each opponent. This leads to close calculation when a choice of suit is involved. In the example given earlier, where a bidder could have named either Diamonds or Spades, he might prefer Diamonds as trump rather than risk a double loss in Spades by stretching it too far.

Hearts Triple is a modern innovation which, as its name implies, means triple stakes whenever Hearts is declared trump. A Heart bid, played and lost, can be a severe jolt to the bidder. By winning a 330 bid in Hearts, he would receive 30 chips from each opponent or 60 in all; declaring Hearts and losing the bid, he would give each 60 chips or 120 in all. Hearts Triple should be included in the game only by previous agreement.

Adding More Players

Additional players may be included in a game of Auction Pinochle, but only three are active in each hand. With four players, one acts as dealer but does not participate. After the hand, the deal moves along to the next player, who simply deals to the others and leaves himself out during that deal.

With five players, two are dealt out, namely the dealer and the player to his left. This continues around the table, with three active and two inactive players during each hand.

All players figure in the scoring; however, if the bidder wins an ordinary 330 bid, he would collect 30 chips, 10 from each of the other players in a four-handed game; or 40 chips in a five-handed game. This increases the stakes in Spades double and Hearts triple proportionately.

Many veteran Pinochle players regard the four-handed game with dealer out, as the ideal form of Auction Pinochle.

III

BIDDING IN AUCTION PINOCHLE

Bidding is really the *name of the game* where Auction Pinochle is concerned. In fact, there are just two big mistakes that a player can make. One is to overbid his hand and the other is to underbid it. Overbidding naturally brings disaster, but in the long run, underbidding will prove just as bad. Where the overbidder loses what he has gained, and often more, because of his eagerness to take control, the underbidder seldom gains enough to matter. Yet such players habitually blame their misfortune on anything except themselves.

The high bidder who doesn't make it can always say that *the right card wasn't in the widow,* or that one opponent had *more than his share* of the trumps. The low bidder who could have gone higher invariably insists that it was *just his bum luck* to have extra counters fall his way when he didn't need them. He is even apt to lay it on poor play by his opponents, rather than wake up to the fact that he doesn't know how to gauge the value of his hand when he makes a bid.

All this can be rectified by using an intelligent *point count system* that can prove remarkably accurate in its estimate, along with calculating the chances offered by the widow, not just in the added points it has to offer, but whether you should rely on the widow at all during that particular hand. Taking all factors in their proper order, your analysis of a hand in Auction Pinochle should include the following heads:

1) The actual meld in the hand as dealt. Basically, this is a fixed amount that can be added at the start, but may require some adjustment later. That, however, depends upon the other factors, so the first step is to add the meld as it stands.

2) This is where the *point count* figures. It consists of adding up the actual counters that you expect to take during the play, along with others that you should acquire by taking extra tricks as the play proceeds.

3) The prospects offered by the widow, which in their turn can be tabulated in relation to the meld and point count, thereby determining whether you should risk depending on the widow and how far you should bank upon it if you do.

From all three factors, a player can determine the *type of bid* he must use, both to outbid his opponents and to weigh the prospects of an increased bid against the risks involved in making it. That classifies all bids in the following categories, all involving the widow:

1) The *Safe Bid,* where the widow is not needed.

2) The *Normal Bid,* where reliance on the widow is always advisable.

3) The *Risk Bid,* where reliance on the widow is occasionally advisable, though sometimes strongly so.

4) The *Wild Bid,* where reliance on the widow is rarely advisable, though sometimes justifiable.

5) The *Bluff Bid,* where the widow is not even wanted, because the sole purpose is to force rival bidders higher.

Point Count and Playing Value

It is a very simple matter to add the potential value of a Pinochle hand to that of the meld, by means of the point count system. Suppose the bidder holds the following hand:

♠: A,K,Q,Q ♥: A,K,K,Q ♦: A,10,J,J ♣: A,10,J

This hand has a sure meld of 220, due to Four Aces (100), two Marriages (20 + 20), and two Pinochles (40 + 40). Since no suit predominates, it is impossible for the player to decide upon a trump until after he has seen the widow, hence both the Marriages (**K♠**, **Q♠** and **K♥**, **Q♥**) must be classed as Ordinary Marriages for the present. This hand has also been selected for analysis because it does not offer a chance of large improvement from the widow, since no single card will benefit the hand.

In short, no wise player ever counts on picking up *two* needed cards from the widow, such as 10, J of Spades or Hearts; or the K, Q of Diamonds or Clubs, which he would have to get in order to fill a Trump Sequence. Similarly, Four Kings or Four Queens would require a two card *fill,* so that is also out. Even catching a second **K♠** to go with the extra **Q♠**, or a second **Q♥** to go with the extra **K♥**, is too unlikely to be given consideration. Such draws are regarded as freaks which are helpful when they do occur, but are pitfalls if taken seriously. So the hand must be considered as it stands, with its sure meld of 220.

Now comes the simple point count that determines the playing value. Each Ace is regarded as a sure trick; therefore count it as 10 points, because if you lead an Ace, neither opponent will throw on a counter if he can help it, so it should only bring 10 points (or 11 by the little-used Original Count, which is close enough). Each Ten may be a winner; the chance of making one good can be figured about even. So each Ten is counted as 5 points. Four Aces (40) and two Tens (10) total 50. Adding the 220 meld, that gives this hand a safe Bidding Value of 270.

To that, some players add a "Widow Value" of 30 points, which would bring the *safe* estimate up to 300. This is based on the fact that anything from the widow should boost the hand's value by 30 points or more, which is usually quite true. But some of those points may be needed as a cushion if snags are encountered during play. Suppose that the player in this case should lead the **A♦** and have it trumped by an opponent who had no Diamonds in his hand; and the opponents then went on to take the player's **10♦** and **10♣**. That would put him 20 points short of his supposedly safe bid.

But if the widow had merely supplied him with the **9♠**, **9♦** and **9♣**, which seem small pickings indeed, he could declare Spades as trump, turning his Plain Marriage (**K♠**, **Q♠**) into a Royal Marriage, giving him 40 points instead of 20 and the **9♠** would become the Dix of the trump suit, for 10 points more.

Another important factor is when the successful bidder picks up the widow, he *automatically* gives his hand at least one five-card suit, if he wants to keep it, which he almost always does. Each card over four in a suit has a potential count of

20 points where playing value is concerned, but here the bidder should make sure that his trumps are strong enough to clear out the opposition, particularly if he is depending on a long side suit.

Many veteran Pinochle players just can't seem to appreciate the potentials of a long suit. To them, a 20-point rating for an insignificant extra card in a side suit sounds preposterous. So to "prove the point," so to speak, let's take a look at the mathematical principles on which the Pinochle Point Count is based. For that purpose, what is properly termed the Ideal Hand in Auction Pinochle:

♠: A,A,10,10,K,K,Q,Q,J,J,9,9 ♥: A ♣: A ♦: A

This hand melds a Double Sequence in Spades, for 150 + 150 with 10 more for each Dix, and Four Aces for 100, making a total meld of 420. Since every trick is a sure trick, the bidder doesn't even have to look at the widow. He can simply lay down the hand, or play it any way he wants, and take in 250 points in play for a grand total of 670.

Suppose, however, that he plays all his Aces first, as is customary with a strong hand and follows with his two Tens of Trumps. Assume that the widow has two counters, as the **10♦** and **K♣**, with a **9♥** as a non-counter; and that the remaining counters are equally divided between the two opponents. What happens then?

THIS HAPPENS: On all five Aces, each opponent plays a worthless card, so all that the Aces bring in are themselves, at 10 points each, *exactly as rated by the point count*. Next, the two Tens of Trumps account for themselves at 10 points each. By the point count, they were rated at 5 points each, but that meant 10 for one and 0 for the other, so this just happened to be a case where both clicked and came through with 10.

So far, seven cards have been played, all sure winners in any hand, yet they have accounted for a mere seven points. There are two snugly tucked away in the discarded widow, making nine in all. But with only *eight more tricks* to be played, that leaves *sixteen counters* still unaccounted for! Or not quite unaccounted for, since the bidder himself has two Kings, which are counters in their own right — 10 each by the Simplified Count, which is being used in this example — but Kings are not usually regarded as trick takers.

This time they are. The bidder plays his first trump, King, and it picks up two non-counters, like the Aces and the Tens did. The next King, however, picks up a counter and a non-counter, so it brings in 20 points, including itself. From then on comes a trump parade of Queens, Jacks and Nines, all non-counters, each bringing in two counters for a total of 20 points, until the final Nine brings in *30 points,* the extra 10 being for Last Trick, which goes to the credit of the first King. That is because all eight of these cards (K, K, Q, Q, J, J, 9, 9) represent the extras *in a long suit.*

Many keen players just can't go along with suit value of 20 points for each extra card, because they have seen many hands where opponents play counters on each other's tricks right from the start. As a result, they think of non-counters as left-overs that are thrown away toward the finish of a hand. That is quite true in hands where the bidder either lacks a long suit or the ability to establish one early enough to prevent his opponents from *smearing* each other's tricks, as the mutual exchange of counters is termed.

Here is a good example of a hand with a long trump and other prospects that invite the bidder to stretch a *Safe Bid* almost to its limit:

♠: A,A,K,Q,Q,9 ♦: 10,Q,J,J ♣: A,A,Q ♥: 10,Q

This hand has a meld of Four Queens for 60, two Pinochles for 40 + 40, a Royal Marriage in Spades for 40, and the Dix (**9♠**) for 10, making a total meld of 190. Its point count is 20 for two Aces of Spades, which many players rate at 25 because of their possible chance of capturing a counter. Also, 20 for the two Aces of Diamonds, which can also be boosted to 25, because of the *Double Ace* as it is termed. Add 5 + 5 for the two Tens and the count so far comes as high as 25 + 25 + 5 + 5 = 60.

Here, a modification is recommended, which simplifies the counting process and can be used with many hands. It is this: Keep each Double Ace at 20, but keep it in mind as a strengthening influence where the widow is concerned. In contrast, in this case, each Ten can be promoted from 5 to 10 in playing value because the **10♦** is protected strongly enough to take a trick, while the **10♥** can probably be put away in the widow discard. So four Aces at 10 each and two Tens at 10 each amount to the same total of 60.

Now comes the suit strength represented by Spades as trump. Since there are two cards more than four, the bidder adds 20 each, bringing the point count up to 100. That brings the total up to 290, but the hand is definitely worth a bid of 300 or a trifle higher. Here is the reason why:

There are six Spades still unaccounted for, and if any one of those should be in the widow, it would add 20 points to the playing value of the hand by increasing the number of Spades from six to seven. Similarly, there are eight Diamonds that would do the same, by putting a fifth Diamond in the hand. Either a **10♠** or an **A♦** would add a playing value of 10, thus being worth 30 points in its own right, while there are seven Kings that would add a Marriage to the meld: **K♦**, **K♦**, **K♣**, **K♣**, **K♥**, **K♥**, at 20 each, with one **K♠** promising 40 points for a Royal Marriage.

The chances are about ten to one that the bidder will pick up a widow that will give this hand an extra 30 points. So it is worth a bid of 300. If an opponent ups that to 310, the hand is worth a bid of 320. Or, if the previous player bid at the 300 level, this hand should be bid at 310. But to go beyond 320 could prove a grievous mistake for this simple reason. Some of the "goodies" gained from the widow may prevent the bidder from discarding enough cards to make room for them. Or, it may cause him to lose something that he already has.

As an example: The bidder picks up **K♣, K♥, 9♦**. That looks fine. Two Marriages (**K♣, Q♣** and **K♥, Q♥**) are good for 40 and the **9♦** stretches the Diamond suit for 20 more. But what can he discard? Only the **10♥**. Otherwise, he will have to nullify part of his original point count or something that he gained. That's not bad. It's good, as a warning not to expect too much from the widow and therefore not to stretch the bid too far.

Summarizing this hand, it still comes into the Safe Bid category, for the obvious reason that there is no great improvement to be gained from the widow, in the way of one card fills. You can't fill a Sequence in either Spades or Diamonds. Four Aces, Four Kings and Four Jacks are hopeless. So the only course is to play it safe and stay within bounds.

Here is a hand that is a true *two suiter* because it already has a fifth card in both Spades and Hearts, a double encouragement toward stretching a Safe Bid too far:

♠: A,A,10,K,K ♥: A,A,K,Q,9 ♦: A,K,Q ♣: A,K

Four Aces are good for 100 points, Four Kings for 80, a Royal Marriage in Hearts for 40, a plain Marriage 20, with 10 for a Dix, making a meld of 250. In point count, Ace, Ace, Ten of Spades can be rated at 35, with the Ten taking on the value of an Ace, while the Double Ace in Hearts can be counted at 25, and the single Aces 10 + 10, for a total of 80. In suit length, Spades and Hearts each have a fifth card for 20 points each, bringing the count to 120. Add that to the 250 meld and the hand is biddable at 370.

The simpler variation is to count each of the six Aces as 10 points, plus the odd Ten at 10, which comes to 70 instead of 80, thereby fixing the bid at 360 instead of 370, which is close enough. Indeed, so close that you would be wise to stop right there without adding anything for widow value, although at first glance, the hand seems heavily loaded in that department. The catch, however, is this:

The hand is so strongly overmelded that no matter what the widow offers, you may have to sacrifice about the same amount in melds or points that you already have. This is a common fault with two-suit hands and this case happens to be a prime example, serving as a reminder that you should always allow for discards when considering widow prospects. So in bidding the hand shown here, you should aim for the 350 level, going to 360 if an opponent named 350 before you, and to 370 if you must, but no higher.

Study the hand closely and you will see that there is nothing you can discard without losing a potential 20 points or more. The spare Ace of Spades is worth 10 as a trick taker and 20 as the fifth card in the suit, which would be a loss of 30 points. The same applies to the Ten of Spades and the spare Ace of Hearts. Dropping one King of Spades would be a loss of 20 points for a fifth card; and dropping the Queen of Diamonds would kill a meld of 20 for a Marriage. Throwing away the Nine of Hearts would mean a loss of 10 points for the Dix and 20 for the fifth Heart.

Picking up the **Q♠** from the widow would be very nice, as you could declare your strongest suit, Spades, as trump, giving you a meld of 40 for a Royal Marriage and 20 for the sixth card in Spades. But that gain of 60 would be cut to 10 because you would have to demote the Heart Marriage from 40 to 20 and the **9♥** would no longer count as a 10 point Dix. If you discarded the **9♥** to make room for the **Q♠**, your gain of 20 points for an extra Spade would be nullified by the loss of 20 for the fifth Heart.

All the widow really offers is the chance to pick up counters and immediately discard them. Using the Simplified Count, your hand already contains twelve counters (Aces, Tens, Kings); leaving twelve to be heard from, which means you can count on 10 points in the widow and might be lucky enough to get 20.

Understand, this is a good hand at the 350 level; its best feature being that it can be gauged so closely, which is all the more reason not to overbid it. The same rule applies to all hands that are too rigid in meld and point count to allow any leeway in the discard.

Here, in contrast, is a hand of more flexibility:

♦: K,K,Q,Q,J,J,9,9 ♠: 10,10,Q ♥: A,A,9 ♣: A

This contains two Royal Marriages for 80, plus 10 for each Dix and a Pinochle for 40, making a total meld of only 140. Hence, this hand requires 110 points in play to meet a minimum bid of 250. Most players would therefore pass it up as an opening bid, due to its total lack of high cards in Diamonds, which is the only plausible trump suit. They could picture themselves taking in 30 points with the Aces and maybe 40 more with four of the trump cards, but that would be about all.

However, by the Point Count System, the hand should be good for 130 in counters and perhaps more, making it worth an opening bid of 250, and even 260 or 270, if somebody else should open. Here is how it adds up: Three Aces and two Tens at 10 each, for 50 points, plus four extra cards in Diamonds at 20 each, for 80, which makes 130.

Why should each Ten count for 10, with only a Queen as a guard against their being taken with two Aces? Because those Tens are earmarked as discards for the widow, making each good for 10 points right there. If you should pick up a couple of lesser counters, like the **K♥** and **K♣**, you could leave them in the widow and add one **10♠**, thus putting away 30 points. If the widow should have another **K♥** or **K♣**, you would leave them there for 30 and try to make one **10♠** good in play.

Of course, if the widow should bring you the **K♠**, you could add it to your hand as a 20-point Marriage and discard the **9♥**, as you would have the **K♠** and **Q♠** to play on opposing Aces, giving you a chance to win with one Ten or both. A nice thing about this hand is that with only three Aces, there are five more in the pack. If one of those showed up in the widow, it would be a sure trick, letting you put away one of your Tens instead; unless it happened to be an Ace of Spades, then you might want to keep the Tens with it.

Your long trump suit in Diamonds is far more powerful than it looks, because even the lowly Nines can be used to force out opposing Aces or Tens. Unless those should all be in one opposing hand, you should take at least five trump tricks, and with lots of counters in opposing hands you would easily pick up all you need.

IV

BIDDING

ON PROSPECTS

If a capable Pinochle player confined his bidding to *Safe Bids* during an all-night session with a couple of equally competent opponents, he could very well find himself the big loser by dawn. That sounds somewhat preposterous, since a *Safe Bid* is very nearly foolproof, yet it is foolish to rely constantly on such bids. In short, a *Safe Bid*, though the surest, is by no means the best if prospects for a bigger gain are really good.

As already stated, such prospects hinge on tne number of fills offered by the widow. In scanning the hand, you look for spaces that can be filled with a missing key card, giving you an additional meld of 60 points or better. If there are three or more possible fills, you would normally bid the additional amount promised by the lowest fill. That is why the term *Normal Bid* is used in such instances.

The chances of making a fill when three spaces are available can be regarded as about even, or a trifle better in some cases where only 60 or 80 additional points are needed for the higher bid. That is because the widow occasionally provides an unexpected break, such as two cards toward a Sequence in a suit you weren't even considering for trump, or two Kings of different suits to go with two others that you already have. A normal bidder never counts on such breaks, but they are part of the overall odds, as will be explained.

In hands with four or more possible fills, the odds are proportionately stronger in the bidder's favor, making the *Normal Bid* all the more attractive. So in the long run, he should win more hands than he loses, all at higher levels than the *Safe Bid* that he would otherwise have made. Furthermore, when playing *Spades Double,* which is standard procedure in most Auction circles, a player can simply throw in his hand without declaring trump if he fails to make his fill. He is then charged with only a single loss. But if the widow gives him a card he needs, he declares Spades as trump and scores a double win when he makes his bid.

Of course, such a player will stay with *Safe Bids* when he has no prospects for a *Normal Bid,* so he will gain his share of those as well. The upshot is that he will continually outbid the player who never ventures beyond the *Safe Bid.* Also, he will profit heavily at the expense of players who habitually go beyond the *Normal Bid,* as their losses will be his gains. By stretching his *Safe Bids* to *Normal Bids,* he often pushes such unwary opponents past their proper limits.

A study of hands and their prospects will bring out some interesting angles pertaining to the *Normal Bid.* For a starter, consider this very unusual hand:

♥: A,K,K,Q,J ♣: A,A,K,Q,J ♠: A,K,Q,J,J ♦: —

This hand has a meld of only 80 points, composed of a Royal Marriage for 40 in whichever suit is finally declared as trump, plus two plain Marriages at 20 each. Its point count is 40 for the Aces (at 10 each) and 20 each for the fifth cards in the three suits, which amounts to 60. Adding 80 + 40 + 60 brings the total to 180, which could be stretched to 200 for a *Safe Bid.*

However, a *Normal Bid* offers very surprising prospects, for this hand has no less than seven possible fills! That means fourteen possible cards (two of each value) out of the thirty-three cards remaining in the pack. Assuming that the player picks up one of his needed fills with two worthless cards, as the **9♦** and **9♦**, here are his possible improvements:

Q♦: 60 points for Four Queens.

J♦: 80 points for Pinochle (40) and Four Jacks (40).

K♦: 80 points for Four Kings.

A♦: 110 points for Four Aces (100) and added point count (10).

10♥: 140 for Trump Sequence.

10♣: 140 for Trump Sequence.

10♠: 140 for Trump Sequence.

Note: In any of the Sequences, the bidder would lose 40 points already allotted to a Royal Marriage, since it would be absorbed into the Sequence, which would add only 110 points instead of 150. But the Ten of Trumps would be worth 10 in point count, plus 20 in added suit length, bringing it up to 140.

This hand has two levels for normal bidding. One would be 250 for filling with the **Q♦**, **J♦**, or **K♦**. The other would be 300 for the **A♦**, **10♥**, **10♣** or **10♠**, though that could be stretched if needed. Actually, the original count of 180, plus 60 for the **Q♦** and its Four Queens, only totals 240; and to keep the **Q♦** means discarding one **K♥**, thus losing 20 points given to Hearts for suit length. That brings it down to 220.

Similarly, if the bidder filled with either the **J ♦** or the **K ♦**, his 180 + 80 = 260 would be reduced to 240. But in each instance, a 250 bid is justified. The rich prospects of the widow, the Double Ace in Spades, the **K ♥** bringing 10 points as a discard, could be good for those needed 30 points, or more.

In a test deal of eleven widows, three cards each from the total of thirty-three, there were nine fills involving the seven key cards listed. Of the other two, one was ♥: A, 9, 9. This enabled the bidder to name Hearts as trump, melding 20 points (10 for each Dix) plus 10 for the **A ♥** and 60 for additional suit length, or 90 in all. Subtracting 40 for loss of suit length by discarding **J♣**, **J♠**, **J♠**, the bidder still made 50. The other widow was **A♠**, **K♣**, **Q ♥**, which brought 30 for the **A♠** (10 in play, 20 for added suit length); 60 for the **Q ♥** (40 for Royal Marriage, 20 in suit length); and 10 for discard of the **K♣**, a total of 100. Also discarded were the **J ♥** and **J♣**, for a loss of 40 points in suit length, giving the bidder a 60 point gain.

So the hand would have been a sure winner at the 250 bidding level.

If an opponent had pushed the bidding to beyond 250, it normally would have gone to the 350 level, and the bidder would have been justified in chancing it at 360 or 370 and maybe 380, if pressed to it. But a 400 bid would have been too risky and too costly if the bidder failed to make it. Remember that the bidder, in going for 350, would still have four possible fills — the **10 ♥**, **10♣**, **10♠** and **A ♦** — giving him eight chances out of the remaining thirty-three cards.

That means *eight possible fillers* — with eleven possible widows — provided none of those eleven trios contain two key cards. Without going into abstruse mathematical calculations, that would mean eight chances out of eleven, which is better than two to one. It runs less than that in actuality, because two keys do have a way of occasionally coming up together. But with the help of freaks, it is generally two to one in the bidder's favor.

In the test deal just described, there were only seven sample widows that contained one of the needed keys, because one trio held the **10♥** twice. That reduced the ratio, making it seven out of eleven, which is less than two to one. But one group of three cards contained, of all things, the **K♦**, **Q♦** and **K♦**, giving the bidder *three* lesser fills that he wasn't counting on where 300 was concerned. Study the result and you will see that he picked up Four Kings for 80, Four Queens for 60, Four Jacks for 40 and a Pinochle for another 40, or a meld of 200 to go along with his initial meld of 80. By discarding his extra **K♥**, **J♠** and one of his Aces, his bid would be so neatly in the bag that there would be no need to play out the hand. Also, a bidder getting an unexpected bonanza like that could simply declare Spades as trump and collect double.

Here is a hand which offers five fills for the bidder, a type that is also seldom seen:

♠: A,10,K,Q ♦: A,K,Q,J ♣: A,10,10 ♥: A,10,K,Q

One nice thing about this hand is its big meld and high point count toward play, which gives the bidder a real good start. In meld, Four Aces bring 100, a Royal Marriage 40, two plain Marriages 40 (20 + 20) and a Pinochle (**Q♠** and **J♦**) 40 making a total of 220. Counting Aces and Tens at 10 gives the hand 80 more for a grand total of 300.

An ultra-conservative bidder might be tempted to let it ride with a Safe Bid at that level, but he would be passing up a powerful opportunity. The hand is definitely worth an immediate shot at the coveted 400 mark, because of its five possible fills:

Q♣: 60 points for Four Queens.
K♣: 80 points for Four Kings.
J♠: 130 points for Trump Sequence.
J♥: 130 points for Trump Sequence.
10♦: 140 points for Trump Sequence.

With the possible Sequences, 40 points have been deducted from 150 for a lost Royal Marriage; but in each case there is an addition of 20 points for a fifth card in the suit, while the **10♦** gathers in 10 more in playing points.

With ten usable cards out of thirty-three that could turn up in the widow, chances could be as high as ten to one in the bidder's favor, but don't expect it to be that good, there are very apt to be two key cards in the widow and occasionally three, when so many fills are possible. In this case, a "test deal" of eleven widows produced eight containing key cards, against three that had none. That's pretty close to two out of three in the bidder's favor. So it's smart to go after it. However:

Based on a *Safe Bid* of 300, the bidder must improve his hand by 100 points to make his 400 bid. The **Q♣** as a filler adds only 60 to his meld. Will that be enough if he has to depend on the **Q♣**?

The same question might also apply to the **K♣** as a filler, since its additional meld of 80 is still short of the needed 100. The answer is that with this particular hand, both the **Q♣** and **K♣** should satisfy the 400 requirement. The reason is that the hand offers ideal discard opportunities. If the bidder fills a Sequence (in Spades, Diamonds or Hearts), he can bury three Tens in the discard.

But if he gets the **Q♣** or **K♣**, what then?

If he gets two other Clubs with it, he keeps one, but buries the other, along with the **10♠** and **10♥**. That gives him 20 points in suit length, since the hand will contain five Clubs, so if he drew the **K♣**, he is all set. If he drew the **Q♣**, he runs a risk, but it is slight and worth the ristk, because:

If he gets one other Club with his **Q♣** or **K♣**, he can keep it and bury the card from another suit; or he can bury his Club instead. That gives him a very valuable choice. For example: He gets the **Q♣**, **J♣**, **K♦**. He keeps the **Q♣** for his 60 points

(Four Queens) and the **J♣** for his fifth Club (20 points) and he buries the **K♦** for another 10 points which it probably wouldn't make in play.

If he gets the **Q♣** with two cards from any other suit, he can bury his two Tens of Clubs and keep a card from one of the other suits, whichever seems best. Either will give him 20 points for suit length, which should be good enough. This is an almost unbeatable hand at 400. The only question now is whether it should go higher. The answer to that is: If necessary, yes.

Bidding higher than 400 on the strength of the **Q♣** or **K♣** would be unwise. But with any of the three possibles toward a Sequence, it would be a good proposition. So if the Normal Bid on the strength of *five fills* should be forced above the 400 level, the bidder could jump it to 450 — which pays off higher if successful — on the strength of his three possible fills in Trump Sequences — **J♠**, **K♦**, and **J♥**.

Here is a nice type of hand that you might be able to pick up once in a while; not too often, yet not too seldom:

♠: A,10,K,Q,Q ♦: A,K,Q,J,J ♣: A,10,Q ♥: K,Q

This gives the bidder a good start, with a Double Pinochle (**Q♠**, **Q♠**, **J♦**, **J♦**) for 80, Four Queens for 60, a Royal Marriage for 40 (trump to be named later) and two Plain Marriages for 40 (at 20 each), a total meld of 220. To that add 50 points for Aces and Tens (at 10 apiece) and 40 for two extra cards. one in each of the two long suits (20 + 20), bringing the total to 310.

This hand has four possible fills, all offering improvement of 100 plus, which is very attractive to the Normal Bidder. The openings are as follows:

K♣: 100 for Four Kings (80) and Plain Marriage (20).

A♥: 110 for Four Aces (100) with playing count (10).

J♠: 150 for Sequence. (Deduction of 20 for lost marriage is offset by added 20 for suit length).

10 ♦: 160 for Sequence (150) and added playing count (10). (Marriage deduction offset by added suit length).

Any of those prospects are worth a jump from a *Safe Bid* of 300 to a *Normal Bid* of 400. The main inducement for a *Safe Bid* of 300, 310 or 320 is that this hand is good enough as it stands, with Spades as trump, thus offering double profit at the 300 level. Almost anything from the widow can add enough more points to clinch it, so why go for more?

Proponents of the Normal Bid will stress that the same prospect applies with a bid of 400, 410 or 420, since Spades can be named as trump with three of the four possible fills. The sole exception is the **10 ♥**, which means naming Hearts as trump; but since the **10 ♥** offers the biggest meld of all, it is worth it. Note here that the game included the feature of *Hearts Triple,* a *Normal Bid* on the chance of catching the **10 ♥** would be an absolute must.

The *four fill* prospect is the most powerful factor in favor of the *Normal Bid,* as such opportunities strengthen the overall percentage in the*Normal Bidder's* favor. Here, there are eight cards that will do for the four fills, out of thirty-three possible cards, so the bidder's chance is as high as 8 out of 11 potential widows. Practically speaking, this drops under 7 out of 11, due to the chances of two keys coming in a single widow, but it still runs to 3 out of 5 or even 2 out of 3 in the bidder's favor.

Here, another question arises in regard to this particular hand: Could the *Normal Bidder* forget the fill offered by the **K♣** and go for 450 on the strength of the other three: **A ♥**, **J♠**, and **10 ♦**? The answer in this case would be "No." The problem is the **A ♥**. It improves the hand by 110, so 30 more would bring it up to 450, which seems likely enough, but the trouble is the discard.

Suppose the widow should produce **A ♥**, **A♠**, **Q ♦**. That brings 110 from the **A♥**, while the **A♠** counts for 30 (with playing value of 10 and suit length of 20). The **Q ♦** comes up with another 20 for suit length, which raises the improvement to 160. But that leaves *only one discard* in the entire hand; namely, the **10♣**. By putting away the extra **Q ♦**, the hand would lose the 20 it just gained from that card; and the only other discard would be the **K ♥**, which would count 10 in the widow, but would cut the meld value by 20 for breaking up the Heart Marriage. Other combinations involving the **A ♥** bring up the same problem. The hand is just too heavy on meld to allow any of the minor improvements that would be needed.

With either the **J♠** or the **10 ♦**, the single fill is sufficient in itself. The other two cards from the widow could be put right back and the **10♣** could be buried with them. In each case, a Sequence would be filled (in Spades or Diamonds) and the original meld and playing value would be preserved intact. But the **A ♥** can be a delusion and a snare for the player who thinks he can snag some extra help with it. He can't with this hand. Hence it is wise to be on guard against tight discards whenever a hand depends on help from the widow.

Now for some varieties of hands with just three possible fills, which should give the *Normal Bidder* slightly better than an even chance of getting what he needs from the widow. These, of course, are the type he runs into most often, but they furnish all sorts of angles. Here is one of the nicest:

♠: A,A,10,Q,9 ♦: A,10,K,J ♥: 10,10,K,Q ♣: A,K

This has a mere meld of 70, formed by the Spade Dix (10), a Plain Marriage (20) and a Pinochle (40), which might cause some players to pass it up. But its playing count of 80 (from Aces and Tens at 10 each) brings its value up to 150, plus 20 more for suit value from the extra Spade; making a grand total of 170. Its potential fills are as follows:

K♠: 140 for Eight Kings (80), a Royal Marriage (40), sixth card in suit (20). (Dix already counted.)

A♥: 130 for Four Aces (100), plus playing value (10), fifth card in suit (20).

Q♦: 170 for Trump Sequence (150) plus fifth card in suit (20).

Taking 130 as the minimum improvement, that makes a *Normal Bid* of 300, but that can be neatly stretched to 310 or 320 due to the opportunities for effective discards. With Spades as trump, the **10♦**, **10♥** and **10♥** can be discarded without detracting from meld or playing value; while with Diamonds trump, the **10♥**, **10♥**, **K♥** and **K♣** are all good discards. If the **A♥** comes in the widow giving the hand Four Aces, practically any other two cards from the widow will boost the value of the hand.

For example, with **A♥**, **9♥**, **9♦** from the widow, the player would keep the **A♥** and **9♥**, gaining 20 points from the **9♦** as an extra card in a long suit. He would also keep the **9♦** and would discard the **10♦**, **K♦** and **K♣**, thus burying three counters, of which two (the **K♦** and **K♣**) would have been sure losers in play, saving him 20 points right there. Anything coming with the **Q♦** can prove equally adaptable to the discard, but when the **K♣** is in the widow, discards may be more difficult, due to the necessity of keeping all Four Kings. Hence, a *Normal Bidder* should hesitate at bidding this hand above 320.

Here, in contrast, is a hand that offers full leeway where melding is concerned:

♠: A,A,K,9,9 ♦: A,K,Q,J ♣: A,10,Q,J ♥: A,10

The present meld consists of Four Aces at 100 and a Marriage in Diamonds for 20; a total of 120. To that, seven Aces and Tens add a point count of 70, while a fifth card in Spades is valued at 10 points; which brings the grand total to 200. Now, in looking for widow prospects, the player immediately sees two possible fills that can bring him a Sequence in either Diamonds or Spades, that would boost the total 150 points. But he needs a third to make a *Normal Bid* and at first glance, it is absent. However, close scrutiny reveals a real sleeper; and he lists his prospects thus:

Q♠: 120 for Royal Marriage (40) Pinochle (40); Two Nines of Spades 20 (10 for each Dix); Extra card in long suit of Spades, (20).

10♦: 180 for Sequence (150) and fifth card in suit (20). Added playing count (10).

K♣: 170 for Sequence (150) and fifth card in suit (20).

Thanks to the almost unsuspected **Q♠**, the bidder can boost his basic count of 200 to 320. But this hand is definitely so strong and its chances of discarding so good, that it is worth 30 more points on added widow power. So, on the basis of three prospective fills, it is worth a *Normal Bid* of 350.

Here are some sample widows involving the **Q♠**, showing ways in which they can be handled to advantage:

Q♠, **Q♦**, **K♥**: Retain **Q♦** for 20 points as extra card in suit. Bury **K♥** for 10, along with **10♣** and **10♥**, clinching them at 10 each.

Q♠, **A♣**, **9♣**: Bury **K♦** and **Q♦**, losing 20 for Marriage. Discard **10♥** with them. Add **A♣** and **J♣** as extra cards to Club suit at 20 each, plus 10 more for **A♣** as playing points. That puts the hand 30 points ahead.

Q♠, **J♠**, **10♣**: Retain **J♠** and add 20 points for extra trump card. Bury **10♣** for 10 points, along with original **10♣** and **10♥**, clinching those as well.

Q♠, **9♦**, **9♦**: Retain **9♦** and **9♦**, adding 40 points for extra suit length. Discard **10♣**, **J♣**, **10♣**.

The last-named widow (**Q♠**, **9♦**, **9♦**) looks trifling, but after the recommended discard, it took 180 points in test play, due to the two long suits (Spades and Diamonds) with the accompanying Aces of Clubs and Hearts. Since the original meld was 120, and the **Q♠** from the widow added another 120 in meld for 240; only 110 was needed to make 350. But all widows aren't that good, so the bid should be kept as close to 350 as possible. With this hand, if either the **10♦** or the **K♣** comes up in the widow, it should be a cinch to win at 350, thanks to the Sequence meld.

Sometimes even a veteran Pinochle player can become too overjoyed when he sorts his hand and finds that it already contains a Sequence and a Dix, putting 160 points in the bag. Add a few Aces to the picture and he is apt to blurt a 300 bid to start, figuring that he is sure to take 140 points in play, which is true. But when the other players let him take it, he is apt to find that what he took for a *Safe Bid* at 300 is worth a lot more as a *Normal Bid,* which he would have gone after if he had checked the prospects carefully. Here is a good example:

♦: A,10,K,Q,J,9 ♠: A,A,K ♥: A,10,Q ♣: 10,K,Q

Right away, the Diamonds glitter with their 160 points. Add a Club Marriage for 20 more, making a total meld of 180. To that, add 70 for playing points (seven Aces and Tens) with 40 for two extra cards in Diamonds. That makes a grand total of 290; enough for anyone to bid 300, as almost anything from the widow can clinch the *Safe Bid.*

Of course, the bidder is sure to see that he only needs an **A♣** to have Four Aces, but he might overlook his chance for Four Kings or Four Queens in his eagerness to make a fast bid. However, if he studies the hand as he should, he would come up with these rather unusual possibilities:

K♥: 100 for Four Kings (80), and a Marriage (20).

A♣: 110 for Four Aces (100) and playing count (10).

Q♠: 120 for Four Queens (60), a Pinochle (40) and a Marriage (20).

Added to the 290 already registered for a Safe Bid, this hand may be good for a *Normal Bid* of 400. The fact that the **K♥** is a bit short (290 + 100 = 390) does not rule it out, because there are two Tens (**10♥** and **10♣**) which can be buried as sure counters. The **K♥** naturally replaces one, but any helpful card from the widow, such as an odd trump, a **10♠** to go with the Double Ace, would aid in the play. If another Heart came from the widow, the bidder could discard the **10♣** and the **Q♣**, sacrificing 20 points for a Marriage, but getting it back in added suit length, which could prove more valuable.

With the **A♣**, which immediately adds playing strength, there are three counters that can be put away in order to keep good cards for play, while the **Q♠** has 20 extra points in meld to carry it over the top. Yet it must be admitted that a hand like this can become a cropper at the 400 level if the trumps are badly divided against it in the other hands.

Therefore, any conservative *Normal Bidder* might prefer to bid this hand at 350, letting himself be forced as high as 370, before taking a chance at 400 — if he would care to chance it even then. The opposing cards may fall right, particularly if one opponent is short of counters that he would like to *smear* on his temporary partner's tricks.

This hand has been specially chosen for analysis at this stage because it represents a transition from the *Normal Bid* to the *Risk Bid,* which is next due for discussion. With three choices, this boosts his bid above the lowest of those potential fills. He is moving from one category to another, even though he may not fully realize it. There is nothing wrong with that; in fact, it is justifiable under certain circumstances for reasons that will become apparent as we proceed.

V

SHOOTING FOR THE MOON

The term ''Shooting for the Moon'' has been used in many games where players take a long chance on something that they should know can seldom come through. Today, people have shot for the moon and made it, but have been glad to get back to earth and take it for what it is. The same thing applies to Pinochle. If you find that you are bidding beyond rational limits, it is time to forget fanciful prospects that fail to materialize. Just gravitate back to earth and stay out of orbit for a while.

That raises the question as to what actually represents sould bidding, or when a bidder should step up the process or restrain it. The answer is variable, depending greatly on the bidding policy of the other players. Once you have determined that, you can decide whether to set the pack or hold back, as well as to the proper degree in each case.

To probe the vagaries of modern Pinochle bidding, consider three players, Andy, Brad and Chet, who are playing a game of Auction Pinochle with standard payoffs of five chips in the 250 to 290 bracket and ten chips in the 300 to 340 bracket. For simplicity, assume that all three are making *Safe Bids* only, so that whoever bids becomes the winner of that deal. In a series of six deals, all these *Safe Bids* fall within the 250 to 290 bracket, never reaching the 300 level.

To simplify it further, suppose that the players make and win their *Safe Bids* in strict rotation, as follows:

ANDY	BRAD	CHET
Safe - Wins 10	Loses 5	Loses 5
Loses 5	Safe - Wins 10	Loses 5
Loses 5	Loses 5	Safe - Wins 10
Safe - Wins 10	Loses 5	Loses 5
Loses 5	Safe - Wins 10	Loses 5
Loses 5	Loses 5	Safe - Wins 10

When added and subtracted, they all come out the same. If that pattern persisted over a prolonged Pinochle session, nobody would win or lose. However, it seldom happens that way. The actual hands will vary greatly, giving opportunities for bigger bids, so if all three players bid correctly and play perfectly, one will come out ahead, simply because Lady Luck sees that he is dealt the most or the biggest winning hands.

Now in the hands just cited, there could have been opportunities for each player to make a *Normal Bid* in every hand, basing such bids on the prospect of three or more spaces in his hand which might be filled from the widow. Assume that these would enable the bidder to jump the bid into the 300 to 340 bracket. None of this showed in the hands already listed, because everybody was satisfied to stay with a *Safe Bid*. But if just one player, Chet, decided to go normal instead of playing safe, here is what could happen:

ANDY	BRAD	CHET
Loses 10	Loses 10	Normal - Wins 20
Wins 10	Wins 10	Normal - Loses 20
Loses 10	Loses 10	Normal - Wins 20
Wins 10	Wins 10	Normal - Loses 20
Loses 10	Loses 10	Normal - Wins 20
Wins 10	Wins 10	Normal - Loses 20

Again, the additions and subtractions cancel out. The only difference is that the stakes have been increased. Again, luck is the big factor, but Chet has two advantages: On hands with more than three chances to fill, the odds are better than even in his favor; and he also profits when he wins a Spades Double. But he also prevents his opponents from making the *Safe Bids* that they would ordinarily win. This is important because:

Suppose that Chet has to stay with his *Safe Bid* in the third and sixth deals because he doesn't have the type of hand needed for a *Normal Bid.* However, he is still able to make a *Normal Bid* in each of the other four hands, thus outbidding *Safe Bids* by Andy and Brad. Here is what would happen:

ANDY	BRAD	CHET
Loses 10	Loses 10	Normal - Wins 20
Wins 10	Wins 10	Normal - Loses 20
Loses 5	Loses 5	Safe - Wins 10
Wins 10	Wins 10	Normal - Loses 20
Loses 10	Loses 10	Normal - Wins 20
Loses 5	Loses 5	Safe - Wins 10

Chet's wins now add up to 60, while his losses are held to 40, giving him a winning margin of 20, while Andy and Brad lose 10 each. The reason, of course, is that he clinched his *Safe*

Bids while gaining a split with his *Normal Bids*. Again, those *Normal Bids* kept his rivals from making the *Safe Bids* that each should have won. So the longer a smart bidder relies on *Normal Bids,* the more he should win, provided that his opponents are strictly *Safe Bidders*. But his winnings are due to the *Safe Bids* that he manages to interject.

Now the nice thing about this system is that the opposing players often fail to grasp its principle. Andy and Brad would soon realize that Chet was outbidding them, but they would be apt to attribute his steady winning to luck and nothing else. To change their luck, they would start outbidding him, hoping that luck would turn their way, only to find that it won't. In short, the player who uses *Normal Bids* may drive his opponents beyond the normal, causing them to lose more than they did with their *Safe Bids*.

However, if the other players fall into the *Normal Bidding* pattern or something close to it, things can even up; like this:

ANDY	BRAD	CHET
Normal - Wins 20	Loses 10	Loses 10
Loses 10	Normal - Wins 20	Loses 10
Loses 10	Loses 10	Normal - Wins 20
Normal - Loses 20	Wins 10	Wins 10
Wins 10	Normal - Loses 20	Wins 10
Wins 10	Wins 10	Normal - Loses 20

Notice that these all balance up with losses offsetting wins Naturally, as the deals continue, there will be numerous times when players will be stuck with *Safe Bids,* but those will cancel out, too. The upshot is that once everybody gets into the act, nobody will win. That's where the *Risk Bid* enters.

RISK BID

The Risk Bid involves a hand with just two openings to fill

instead of the three required for a *Normal Bid.* A good example is the following:

♦: A,K,K,Q,Q,9,9 ♠: Q,J ♥: A,10,J ♣: A,10,J

This hand has a meld of only 100, consisting of two Royal Marriages (40 + 40) and two Nines of Trumps (10 + 10). It has a point count of 50 for five Aces and Tens, plus 60 for three extra cards in the trump suit, Diamonds. That brings its present worth up to 210; not really enough to warrant an opening bid of 250. However, it has two possible fills, which are:

A♠: 110 points for Four Aces (100) and added point count (10).

J♦: 100 points for Four Jacks (40), Pinochle (40) and as seventh card in the suit (20).

Either of these is worth a bid of 300, but since there are only four cards (two each of **A♠** and **J♦**) that would provide the additional meld, the odds at best are only about one out of three (actually 4 out of 11) that the bidder will be able to make it. So if he bid on hands like this all evening, he would lose twice what he made. That's why it's called a *Risk Bid,* which means that it's not worth the risk of a 300 bid.

That is, not ordinarily. But suppose the game has reached the stage where the players are continually outbidding one another, apparently exceeding *Normal Bids.* An opponent opens the bidding at 250 and the player holding this hand boosts it to 300, hoping the opponent will go higher with a bad bid of his own. If the opponent does, he will probably lose the hand. If he doesn't, the player who made the *Risk Bid* at least stopped the opponent from winning the hand at 250; and if he catches a key card from the widow, he may make his *Risk Bid* good as well.

Here is a hand that offers an added opportunity for the *Risk Bidder:*

♦: A,10,K,J,J ♠: 10,K,K,Q,Q ♥: A,J ♣: A,Q,9

This hand melds 120, consisting of two Pinochles for 80 (40 + 40) and two Plain Marriages for 40 (20 + 20). It has a point count of 50 for five Aces and Tens (at 10 each) and 40 for fifth cards in Diamonds (20) and Spades (20). That brings the total to 210. It has two possible fills, which are:

Q♦: 170 points for Sequence (150) and a sixth card in the trump suit, Diamonds (20).

A♠: 170 points for Four Aces (100), 40 for two Royal Marriages (promoted from Plains — 20 + 20 — to Royals — 40 + 40), 10 for playing value of **A♠**, which also adds a sixth card to suit (20). In this case, Spades is trump.

Again, this is a hand that could fall short of 250 as a *Safe Bid,* but if opposing players should open with 250 or even 300, it could be jumped to 350 as a *Risk Bid.* Its original appraisal of 210, plus its two possibilities of 170 come to 380, which should make it an easy winner at 350 or even 360. The trouble is it has only two possible fills, which put it in the *Risk Bid* class.

Assuming that the opponents are in an overbidding mood, a smart player could coax them up from 300 to the 350 level, even pushing one or the other up to 400. If stuck with it at 350 or 360, he would have to take his chances. However, in this case, a *Risk Bid* is better than usual, because:

With Spades Double, this hand would be a big winner if the bidder picked up either Ace of Spades in the widow. He has only two chances in eleven, or about one out of five or six of getting it, but those are the possibilities that make a *Risk Bid* a good gamble, when everyone is bidding beyond the *Normal* limit.

When playing both Spades Double and Hearts Triple, special opportunities crop up where the Risk Bid is concerned, as witnessed by this striking hand:

♠: A,10,K,J,9 ♥: A,10,K,Q,9 ♣: A,10,J ♦: A,J

Here you view an existing meld of 130, formed by Four Aces (100), a Plain Marriage (20) and a Dix (10) in either Spades or Hearts, the two suits that offer prospects of a fill. The point count is 70 for Aces and Tens, plus 40 for fifth cards in Spades and Hearts (20 + 20), so that meld and playing values combined come to 240. The hand has these prospects for a Risk Bid:

Q♠: 210 for Sequence (150), Pinochle (40), extra card in suit (20).

J♥: 190 for Sequence (130, deducting loss of Plain Marriage), Four Jacks (40), extra card (20).

If either space should be filled, this hand should easily hit 400 and some over-optimistic players might figure it at 450, but that could be unwise, because with Hearts as trump, the discard would be too tight to take advantage of additional help from the widow. Taking 400 as a sure shot, the inducement here is that although the odds are two to one against filling the hand, the bidder can only lose 20 chips to each player if he fails to fill; whereas, if he picks up the **Q♠**, he will collect 40 chips, doubled, for a total of 80 chips; and if he picks up the **J♥**, he will collect 40 chips tripled, for a total of 120 chips.

Despite that rosy picture, the bidder should remember that if he loses this hand, he would need two more just like it in order to win one with a Spades Double and thus break even on the three. By the same law of averages, it would take another three hands to win a Hearts Triple and make a profit. But how often is a player dealt a hand that offers a *Risk Bid* at the 40 or 45 level, with possible fills in both Spades and Hearts? Probably so seldom that it would take a player two or three Pinochle sessions to climb out of the hole.

A rational way to bid this hand would be to start at the 250 level, going to 260 if an opponent bids 250 before you; or 270, if both bid 250 and 260 ahead of you. This is a *Safe Bid* in the

250 to 290 bracket, because if you don't catch either the **Q♠** or the **J♥**, you can name Hearts as trump anyway, turning the Plain Marriage into a Royal Marriage for an additional 20 points, giving you a basic estimate of 260 (instead of 240). You can depend on the widow for at least 30 more points with a hand like this, because there are three immediate discards (**10♣**, **J♣**, **J♦**) that could make way for something better.

If you were forced to go to 300, it would still be worthwhile because the widow might bring enough to make it. Then, after picking up the widow, you can decide whether to play the hand or not. For example, a widow combination like **A♠**, **9♥**, **9♦** would be good for 60 points; **10♠**, **K♥**, **K♦**, for 70; and **K♦**, **K♣**, **J♣** would produce Four Kings for 80 points. Such possibilities would give a 300 bid the status of a *Normal Bid* which would be preferable to a *Risk Bid.* If an opponent should keep on bidding, it might be worthwhile to prod him to the 350 level, hoping that your *Risk Bid* would come through even if you should be stuck with it at 340. A loss in the 300-400 bracket wouldn't be too hard to make up later, but to go higher would make it tougher.

Summarized, the *Risk Bid* bears about the same relation to the Normal Bid that the Normal Bid bears to the Safe Bid, with this exception: You can break even with *Normal Bidding* while opponents are holding to *Safe Bidding*. But if you go for *Risk Bids,* you can be sunk by *Safe Bids*. So while it is a good policy to set the pace with *Normal Bids,* it is usually better to leave that to the opposition when *Risk Bids* are involved.

WILD BID

Beyond the *Risk Bid* lies the *Wild Bid,* so called because the bidder is banking on one lone fill from the widow. You will probably never meet a Pinochle player who makes a *Wild Bid* at every opportunity, because anyone doing so could not afford to keep on playing Pinochle. But even players who ignore the promise of a Wild Bid, will sometimes go all-out for this horrible example:

♠: A,10,K,J,9,9 ♦: A,Q,J ♣: A,K,Q ♥: A,10,Q

With Spades as trump, this hand has a meld of 140 formed by Four Aces (100), two Nines of Trumps (20), and a Plain Marriage (20). Its point count is 60 for Aces and Tens, plus 40 for two extra cards in Spades. Its total worth of 240 makes it an ideal *Safe Bid* at 250 with Spades Double, since there are four potential discards (**Q♦, J♦, 10♥, Q♥**) that can make way for another Ace, an extra trump, a couple of counters that might be buried, or a **K♦** or **K♥** toward another Plain Marriage, with the possibility of a fourth and fifth card in a side suit.

However, some players are apt to banish all thoughts of a *Safe Bid* when they see what one missing card will bring, which is:

Q♠: 270 for Sequence (150), Four Queens (60), Pinochle (40), extra card in trump (20).

Add the original 240 to the speculative 270 and it brings a total of 510, making this a sure-fire winner with a bid of 500 which would be good for 120 chips in Spades Double, or even more, if the game is being played by a scoring system where payments take bigger jumps beginning with the 400 level. (See Scoring Schedules, page 000). Thoughts of such a vista may compel a player to make a *Wild Bid* "just this once," although his chances of getting a **Q♠** in the widow are only 2 out of 11, or approximately 1 in 5½.

The odd thing is that such players seldom regret their mistake. They argue that since a loss merely means paying 30 chips to each by throwing in the hand without naming trump, it was something of a bargain after all. If they ran into a few such hands during an evening's play, they would realize their mistake, but such hands are too few and far between to drive the message home.

The other type of player who victimizes himself is the slow but steady loser who moves from the *Normal Bid* into the *Risk Bid* class and then finds himself making a *Wild Bid,* thinking that a few more points will take care of themselves. Here is a type:

♠: A,A,10,10,Q,Q,9 ♦: K,Q,Q,J ♣: A,Q ♥: A,K

With all those Spades as trump takers, it's hard to realize that this hand isn't worth a *Safe Bid* of 250, but it just makes it as a *Normal Bid.* It has a meld of 70, consisting of a Pinochle (40), a Marriage (20), and a Dix (10). Add 60 playing points for Aces and Tens, plus 60 for three extra trumps and it totals 190. There are three possible fills:

K♣: 60 for Royal Marriage (40) and 20 for suit length.

Q♥: 80 for Four Queens (60) and Heart Marriage (20).

A♦: 130 for Four Aces (100), 10 for playing points and 20 for fifth card in Diamonds.

So the player bids 250 and when an opponent makes it 300, the bidder realizes he is beyond the limit of a *Normal Bid,* as represented by the **K♠**. But the Spades are so strong, he decides to go for a *Risk Bid,* in hope of winning Spades Double. So he looks at his best possibility for a fill, the Ace of Diamonds, with its potential meld of 100 and its 30 extra points in playing value.

Then, he figures that the Queen of Hearts would bring a meld of 80, which is only 20 less than the Ace of Diamonds. But there will be other cards in the widow, too, like an odd Ace, worth 10 in play, an extra trump, good for 20, or a couple of counters that might be buried at 10 points each. So he bids 310 in terms of widow value, thinking he is still making a *Risk Bid,* but he isn't. He is making a *Wild Bid,* for this reason:

If he gets the **A♦**, there are three cards he can bury from his hand, without breaking up a meld or losing suit length in Diamonds; namely, the **K♥**, **Q♣**, and the extra **Q♦**. He buries the **K♥** anyway and if he picks up a playable card, he keeps it instead of the **Q♣**. That makes the **A♦** dependable enough for a 320 bid or higher if he had been forced to it.

But such optimism would be wasted on the **Q♥**. He has only one discard, the odd **Q♦**. He can't bury the **Q♣** because he needs it for his Four Queens and he must keep the **K♥** to go with the **Q♦** for the new 20-point Marriage. Anything helpful from the widow, with the exception of the **Q♥**, would have to stay right here and would merely bring his hand up to the 100 mark; no more.

For example: **Q♥**, **10♣**, **10♥**. He would bury the odd **Q♦** along with the **10♣** and **10♥**. His added meld would bring the worth of the hand from 190 up to 270, but the buried counters would add only 20 points more, still short of the 310 bid. The same would apply even with cards like the odd **A♣** or the odd **A♥** if they turned up in the widow. A notable exception would be a freak widow such as **Q♥**, **K♠**, **J♦**, which would bring a meld of 80. Adding 20 for an extra card in Spades, it would be worthwhile to discard the **K♦** and **K♥**, losing 20 each from their respective Marriages. Of course, if both Kings of Spades should come in the widow, along with the Dix, that would be a meld of 90 with 60 more in suit length, so the bidder could forget his Four Queens. But such things just aren't likely to happen.

The more you study your bidding, the more you will realize how the bids can merge from one type into another: *Safe* into *Normal, Normal* into *Risk, Risk* into *Wild.* To keep within the proper limits is the basis of sound bidding and the *Wild Bid* is beyond all limits.

BLUFF BID

Bluffing can play an important part in Pinochle bidding, but it is worthy of its name only when it is done in a purposeful or intelligent manner or when the bluffer stands to gain his end by something more than mere luck. Often, you may encounter players who try to speed the game by bidding on nothing, or pushing the bidding sky-high. They think that they are bluffing, and in a sense they are; but the players they are bluffing are themselves. Very soon, keen players catch on to such antics and simply go about their own bidding in a methodical manner, practically ignoring the self-styled bluffer. He may cut them out of some good bids, but if they stay with *Normal Bidding,* they will profit in the long run.

The true Bluff Bid is something else again. It falls into two categories, or a combination of both. The first has already been partly discussed under the head of the *Risk Bid* and therefore can be applied to the *Wild Bid,* as a form of *Bluff Bid.* One use of the *Risk Bid* is to step up the bidding to higher levels, when you find the trend is in that direction, but ordinarily, it is wise to stop short of the *Wild Bid.* However, when opposing players are obviously overbidding their hands, it is a good policy to encourage them in that procedure. To do this at random may not only prove to be a boomerang, but if your opponents begin to tighten up, they will soon see that you are failing to make any of your overbids and thus catch on to your game.

The correct rule here is to make your bluffs only when you have a hand offering a *Risk Bid* at a higher level than you would ordinarily bid with such a hand; or when you have a *Wild Bid,* particularly in Spades, at almost any level. The same would apply with Hearts, when playing Hearts Triple. The idea here is that you do not expect any of these bids to come through, because your sole objective is to force your rivals higher.

If you succeed in that, their losses should exceed yours, because you would all be losing more bids than you won, but you would be stuck with a bad bid on fewer occasions. So by keeping those bluffs within the range of a *Wild Bid,* or better still, that of a *Risk Bid,* you would not only profit from a few unexpected wins, but would impress your opponents with the fact that your bids were valid.

That covers the first type of *Bluff Bid.* The other is a kind that you can not hope to win, but which can prove even more disastrous for the player who outbids you. Here is a very fine example of such a hand:

♦: A,A,Q,Q, ♣: K,K,9,9 ♥: K,K,9 ♠: Q,Q,9,9

This is what the average player would call a nothing hand, because it hasn't any meld beyond 20 for two Nines of Trump. Its only prospects are quite a few Marriages — two in each suit — and a couple of Pinochles (**Q♠** and **J ♦**) if you can pick up the Jacks to go with them. But — would you believe it! — the chances that the opposing hands will have anything are actually worse than yours.

Study this hand and you will see why. No other hand can hold Four Aces for 100 points, because you have two in one suit, Clubs. They have no chance for Four Kings or Four Queens. You have two identical cards in each suit, making it impossible for another player to be holding a Trump Sequence. Even a Pinochle is out for them, because you have both Queens of Spades. The biggest thing they could have would be Four Jacks for 40 points. Yet it is possible for an opponent to hold a hand that appears to be loaded with prospects, as:

♠: A,A,10,K,J ♥: A,A,10,Q,J ♣: A,10,Q,J ♦: J

This hand looks like a Pinochle player's dream. Although it only has a meld of 40 for Four Jacks, it has *four* possible fills, representing the *highest* prospects: Four Aces and three potential Trump Sequences. It has a point count of 80 (for Aces and Tens) with 40 for extra cards in Spades and Hearts; but with A, A, 10 in the two long suits, it is worth 20 more and the widow should bring at least 40 points from extra cards in Spades, Hearts or Diamonds. That brings it to 220, without making a fill.

So if the player should pick up the **A ♦** from the widow, he would add 100 points and maybe more. Thus, his initial bid should be 300 or maybe 350. Most players would go instantly for 350, because there are *three chances* for a fill of 150 instead of 100, with the **Q♠**, **K♥**, or **K♣** clinching a Trump Sequence, all within the range of a *Normal Bid*. There are players who would shoot for 400 with a *Risk Bid,* because Spades and Hearts are the long suits and a fill in either of those would make it stronger.

Yet anyone holding this hand would probably fall short of making a minimum bid of 250!

That's due to the hand shown previously with its *blockers* that kill every possible combination except Four Jacks. Without those, a rival bidder couldn't even make 200 in play.

So if you should ever find yourself with a *blocker* hand like the one shown, your opening bid should be 250. One or both of your opponents would be almost sure to go higher and you should bow out immediately, because you will know that they can't make whatever they bid and also that you couldn't possibly make your bid either. That's why it comes under the head of a *Bluff Bid*.

The same applies to many hands that show similar earmarks. Seldom will you find one so nearly "pat" that your opponents have practically no chance whatever of filling a worthwhile meld, but by counting your own blockers you can often gauge those chances. If you have Sequences blocked in two suits and also can stop Four Aces, you can be pretty sure that anyone who can be pushed up to 350 is going after one of the two remaining Sequences and is therefore making a *Risk Bid.*

Oddly, Pinochle players are usually so eager to weigh their own chances that they seldom stop to analyze an opponent's. If they studied their poor hands as keenly as they do their good ones, they would find that the opportunities for bluff are just as strong in Pinochle as in Poker and sometimes even better. Just remember that if a bidder needs certain cards, he can't win a high bid unless he gets them; and if you've got them, he can't get them. That's the big key to the *Bluff Bid* in Pinochle.

VI

PLAYING THE HAND

After bidding, taking up the widow, melding and discarding, the play of the hand is in order. In Auction Pinochle, the bidder leads to the first trick, but before launching himself on that mission, he should reappraise his hand to see if he wants to play it at all. This was discussed earlier, when it was stated that the bidder can bow out gracefully, if he feels that his hand can't meet demands. That can happen if he stretches a Safe Bid a trifle too far, particularly when he picks up a widow that proves to be an absolute dud, without any of the help that the bidder had a good right to expect.

This reappraisal is generally rather simple, as the player should have added up his meld and point count before bidding, hence the cards from the widow may fit in the hand automatically or demand immediate rejection. There are times, however, when the choice of a discard is highly arbitrary and even tricky, so special care should be taken in such cases. Whatever his choice, easy or difficult, he must be prepared to adopt a recommended pattern of play before deciding to go ahead.

If his reappraisal indicates that he will fail to make his bid, he can throw in his hand as already stipulated, paying each opponent the amount required by his bid, rather than go ahead and lose in play, which will cost him double, or quadruple if Spades are trump. The question of whether or not to play can therefore loom to prime importance where a high bid is involved and it should be weighed accordingly, to decide if the balance is in your favor.

This is well illustrated by the sample hands that follow, each being shown after the discard, which should be made before the meld is taken back into the hand.

♠: A,10,K,Q,J,9,9 ♦: A,A,10,10,J,9 ♣: J ♥: J

Discard: **10♣, K♥, 9♥**

Assuming that the hand was dealt as shown, the bidder would have simply picked up the widow and then turned it down, since he was bidding on the strength of his pat hand. His meld consisted of a Spade Flush with Nines, for 170; a Pinochle (**Q♠** and **J ♦**) for 40; Four Jacks for another 40, making a total meld of 250. His point count gave him 60 for Three Aces and three protected Tens, plus 60 for three extra Spades (over four) and 40 for two extra Diamonds, a total count of 60 + 60 + 40 = 160.

This added up to 390, so he stretched the bid to 400 in order to reach the higher payoff level. This was justified by the fact that the remaining cards in the pack included nine Spades and Diamonds, plus thirteen counters in other suits. Two counters came with the widow (**10♣** and **K♣**), so he included them in his reappraisal, giving him a count of 410.

Now for a moment of pause, because:

The traditional method of determining how many counters can be won is to check the tricks that the bidder is apt to lose, allocating counters to those. A player using that method could thereby size this hand as follows: Four possible losers in Spades (**Q♠**, **J♠**, **9♠**, **9♠**); two losers in Diamonds (**J ♦**, **9 ♦**); one in Clubs (**J♣**) and one in Hearts (**J ♥**). That adds up to eight losers, none of which are counters, but if the opponents, in taking those tricks, should put two counters on each loser, they would take 160 in counters, utterly defeating the bid.

Here is a real discrepancy: By the modern point count, the bidder should take 140 in play; by the old loser count, he would only take 90, since his opponents feel reasonably sure of 160. Why this variance?.

The answer is simply that the bidder, because of his high cards and two long suits, is sure to take most of those supposedly losing tricks, unless the distribution of the cards in the opposing hands is fantastically freakish. He already has eight counters as winners in his hand, including last trick, plus the two he stowed in the widow, so his opponents have only fifteen to play between them. What's more, unless those were perfectly divided, one opponent would run short of counters to throw on his partner's tricks.

The best way to settle this and prove that the bidder using the point count is right, is to play out the hand and observe what is likely to happen.

Andy, as bidder, leads the **A♠**. One opponent, Brad, puts on the **K♠**; the other, Chet, a **J♠**. Right away, Andy knows the five opposing trumps were dealt three in one hand, two in the other; or four in one hand, one in the other. Andy leads a **Q♠**. Assuming that Brad holds an **A♠** and **10♠**, Andy's **Q♠**

forces the **10♠** and Chet throws on his **Q♠**.

Note: In leading the **Q♠**, Andy hoped that the player holding the lone trump would have either the **A♠** or the **10♠**. In that case, Andy's **Q♠** would have forced both the **A♠** and **10♠**.

From here, Brad and Chet take two tricks with an **A♣** and an **A♥**, adding two counters, as the **K♣** and **K♥**, while Andy throws on his **J♣** and **J♥**. When another **A♣** is led, Andy trumps it with a **9♠**. He then leads his other **9♠**, forcing Brad to take it with the **A♠**, while Chet adds a counter such as the **10♣**. Whatever Brad leads next, Andy takes it with a trump. Andy then uses four high Diamonds to clear that suit and takes the remaining tricks with his two low Diamonds and his trumps.

All that Brad and Chet take between them are seven counters (A's, 10's, K's at 10 points each) for a count of 70, while Andy takes a total of 180, which was thirty more than he needed to make his bid of 400.

Now, suppose that Brad had held *four* of the opposing trump; **A♠**, **10♠**, **K♠**, **Q♠**, with Chet holding only the **J♠**. What then? In that case, Andy would have led the **A♠**, taking the **Q♠** and **J♠**. From then on, Andy would have lost the **Q♠** to Brad's **K♠**, with Chet adding a counter, say the **K♦**. Brad and Chet would have taken their two tricks with the **A♣** and **A♥**, with a **K♣** and **K♥** as counters. After regaining the lead, Andy would have used one **9♠** to force Brad's **10♠**, with Chet adding the **10♣**. Andy would again have regained the lead and used his other **9♠** to force Brad's **A♠**, with Chet adding another **10♣**. After that, all the tricks were Brad's.

Total the counters that Brad and Chet took — **K♠**, **K♦**, **A♣**,**K♣**,**A♥**,**K♥**,**10♠**,**10♣**,**A♠**,**10♣** — and you will see there are just ten, giving them 100 points. So Andy would have taken fifteen for the 150 points he needed to make his 400 bid.

Andy had two reasons for leading trumps so steadily. He had seven of them, making Spades his dominant suit; and he wanted to win tricks with all his high Diamonds, which he could only do by clearing the trumps first. But if circumstances had been only slightly different, Andy would have preferred to do it the other way about, leading his strong side suit first. In fact, Andy did play a hand like that against his same cronies, Brad and Chet. It went like this:

♠: A,10,K,Q,J ♥: A,10,10,Q,J,9,9 ♣: A,J ♦J

Discard: **10♦, K♦, 9♦**

The hand, as originally dealt, contained the **9♦** instead of the **10♠**. It had a meld of 120, composed of a Royal Marriage in Spades (40), a Pinochle (40), and Four Jacks (40). Nevertheless, Andy made a *Normal Bid* of 350 on the strength of three possible fills, the **10♠**, **K♥** and **A♦**. The original hand had a point count of 50 for five Aces and Tens, with 60 for suit length in Hearts. The **10♠** added 110 in meld, 10 for point count and 20 for an extra Spade.

Added up: Total Meld, 230. Point Count, 60. Suit Length, 80. Grand Total: 370.

That would have meant taking 140 points in counters, but Andy picked up the **10♦** and **K♦** in the widow and laid them away for 20 points (by Simplified Count), discarding the **9♦** with them. So he only had to make 120 points in play, but that looked rather tough, because the **10♠** wasn't the draw that Andy wanted most.

The **K♥** would have given him a Sequence plus a Double Dix, with a long, strong trump suit The **A♦** would have added 100 in meld, with 20 for point count and by declaring Hearts as trump, the 20 for the Double Dix would have been included, with the benefit of that long, strong trump suit of Hearts.

Here is why Andy's task looked tough:

With only five cards in the trump suit, Spades, it is all but impossible to clear trumps by leading Spades and still be able to regain the lead in order to win tricks in Hearts. This hand represents a reversal of the one shown earlier, for there, trumps predominated as the longer of the two main suits. Here, it is the other way about: Spades, the trump suit, is two cards shorter than Hearts. So the answer is to reverse the mode of play, by using Hearts to force out trumps from the rival hands.

As an important adjunct to that procedure four of the Hearts are low in value, which means that there will be no waste of counters if they are used as forcers. So here is how Andy goes about it:

Andy leads the **A♥** and takes the **J♥** from Brad, the **K♥** from Chet. Next, Andy leads a **9♥**, Brad puts on a **K♥** and Chet takes the trick with the **A♥**. Chet leads the **A♦**, winning Andy's **J♦** and a **10♦** from Brad; but when Chet leads the other **A♦**, Andy takes the trick with the **K♠**. There goes one of the precious Spades that Andy needs for trumping purposes, but Andy isn't worried — not just yet. He has accounted for four of five Hearts that are out against him, so another Heart lead will force a trump.

Andy leads the **9♥**; Brad plays the **Q♥**; Chet trumps with the **K♠**. Right away, Chet comes back with another low Diamond, which Andy is forced to trump with his **J♠**, and Brad throws on a counter, the **K♦**, which means that Brad is about out of Diamonds. But Andy is more concerned with Hearts. Since Brad and Chet are *both* out of those, they will have to trump Andy's next Heart lead, so Andy will be forcing two trumps instead of only one. So Andy leads the **J♥**, Brad puts on the **A♠** and Chet adds the **9♠**, with Brad taking the trick.

That sudden appearance of the Spade Ace could have been a shocker for a less experienced player than Brad. This could mean that the Ace is Brad's *only* trump, which would show that Chet had six to start with and now has *four* as opposed to Andy's *three,* which could prove fatal to Andy's hopes. But Andy keeps his cool and reasons accordingly that Brad was more likely to have two Spades instead of only one. If so, he played his Ace rather than leave it unprotected, for when the lead gets back to Andy, he could lead the Ace that he melded with his Sequence and thus take Brad's Ace. But why couldn't Brad have taken the trick with his lesser trump and then led the **A♠**? Simply because if he did, he would draw a trump from Chet, which would be all the more to Andy's advantage.

So Andy sits back hopefully while Brad leads the **A♣**, taking a **K♣** from Chet and the **J♣** from Andy. Then comes the break that Andy wants. Brad leads the **9♣**, Chet puts on the **J♣** and Andy takes the trick with his **A♣**. Here, Brad's proper lead would have been a Diamond, as Andy has been trumping that suit all along. But as Andy thought, Brad is *out of Diamonds* and has only *Clubs to play,* except perhaps for a Spade that he won't play.

The important thing is this: Thanks to Andy's Ace of Clubs, he has regained the lead *without using a trump,* which will give him the jump on his rivals, but only if Brad still has a trump in hand. So Andy wastes no time in leading the **Q♥**, the last low one in the suit. On it, Brad plays the **9♠**, the little lurker that Andy wants to see, and Chet takes the trick with the **10♠**. From then on, the show is all Andy's. He has three Spades, Ace, Ten and Queen; while Chet has only two, the Ten and Jack.

Naturally, Chet leads a **Q♦**, forcing Andy to trump it with the **Q♠**, while Brad throws on a low Club. That evens the trumps at two each, but Andy doesn't have to force trumps any more, because his two are the biggest. Andy leads the **A♠** and **10♠**, taking Chet's **Q♠** and **10♠**. That clears the trumps and makes

Andy's high Hearts good. He leads one **10♥**, then the other, picking up all the rest of the cards to complete the play.

Counting the counters after this deal, Andy finds he took 150 in play (by Simplified Count) with 10 more for Last Trick and two extras that he buried in the widow. So he came in nicely over his quota, but it took some neat headwork to do it. The crux was the Club lead that Brad was forced to make to Andy's Ace, but even there, more than mere luck was involved. Some players might have led the **A♣** at the very start, thinking that it meant just another routine trick. But not our Andy. He figured that it might serve as a timely reentry and he kept it for that purpose.

For a real sleeper, here is a hand that actually nonplussed the player who held it. It is included here because it gives some good highlights on the play of a Pinochle hand.

♠: K,K,Q,Q,J,J,9,9 ♦: J,9 ♥A,A,10,Q ♣: A

Discard: **10♦**, **10♦**, **K♣**

The original hand had the **10♦** and **10♦** instead of the **Q♥** and **9♦**. In fact, it was the duplication of the Tens of Diamonds and Aces of Hearts that made the player study the Spades and note that Kings, Queens and Jacks were duplicated, too. Otherwise, he would have passed up the hand as worthless, but now he realized that it was perfect for a Bluff Bid.

One opponent bid 250 and the next made it 260, so our player upped it to 270, wondering how long he should keep raising it step by step. He found out sooner than he expected, when they let him have it at 270. When he turned up the widow and found only the **K♣**, **Q♥** and **9♦**, he was about to throw in his hand when he checked it and found to his surprise that it was playable by the Point Count system.

First, the meld: With Spades as trump, there were two Royal Marriages for 80 and two Nines for 20, plus a Pinochle at 40, making a total of 140. Three Aces and three Tens gave a playing count of 60. The real surprise was the suit value: Four Spades over the normal four, which at 20 points each, added up to 80. There it was: 140 + 140 for meld and play and by discarding the **K♣**, the player put away 10 more points. So since his bid was only 270, he decided to chance it with Spades Double, even though he couldn't believe it. With all those peewee trumps, the only course was to use them and here is what happened:

The bidder led his lone **A♣** as standard procedure; then he led a **9♠** and forced out a **10♠** and **A♠** from his opponents. One took two tricks with two Aces of Diamonds on which the other played two Kings. The next lead was the **A♣**, which our man trumped and got a worthless Club along with it. The bidder then led his other **9♠**, forcing one player to take it with the **A♣**, while the other threw on a counter from a side suit. Back came a low Club, which our man trumped with a **J♠** and led the other **J♠**, forcing out the **10♠**, which gave the opponents another counter as well.

But the end was now in sight. The bidder trumped the next lead and since the opponents were out of trump, he calmly took three tricks with his **A♥**, **A♥** **10♥**; then threw the **Q♥** to the wolves, one taking it with a **10♥** and the other smearing it with a **10♣**. The bidder then took the two last tricks with his remaining trumps.

The count came to exactly 130 by the Simplified Count (A = 10, 10 = 10, K = 10), but it made 140 by the Popular Count (A = 10, 10 = 10, K = 5, Q = 5). So the astonished bidder made his 270. He would have been more astounded if he had reached the 300 mark, which he could very easily have done if one of the four top Spades had been in the widow. The odd **J♦** would have given him another Pinochle; and the other **10♥** would have given him an extra trick in Hearts.

Summarizing the Bidder's Play

Leading out trumps to clear them from opposing hands is ideal when strength and length are in abundance. Otherwise, it is best to utilize a long side suit to draw out opposing trumps until the bidder's hand is dominant. Occasionally, however, the long side suit is too weak to be dependable; then, trump leads become essential. Also there are times when the hand has no long side suit. In order to meld a Double Marriage of four cards in one side suit, a bidder may be forced to put three cards from another suit into the widow, thus shortening what should have been his long side suit. Then, trump leads may become the only answer.

As to trump leads, even experts disagree. Most concede that with a long trump suit headed by an Ace-Ten, it is rather smart to lead the Ace; then switch to a Queen or Jack. The Ace softens the opposition; the next lead, a Queen or Jack, forces out their high trumps. Very good. So some go farther, saying to open with a lead of the Queen and thus force your rivals to play their big ones. But suppose an opponent is shifting unhappily in his seat because he is holding a lone Ace of Trumps, which he will lose if the bidder leads *his* Ace of Trump, which he *showed* when he melded a Trump Sequence.

To the opponent's relief, the bidder leads a Queen instead of an Ace and the opponent promptly clobbers it with his Ace, wondering why the bidder was so dumb that he didn't know that you should always lead an Ace to see what it might bring. If you, as a bidder, ever have the harrowing experience of leading a Queen (or Jack) from a big, long, strong trumps suit, only to have it clobbered by an isolated Ace, one thing will be certain:

You will never again lead a low card instead of an Ace. You will want to feel out the situation before you commit yourself;

and no matter how many experts tell you that you are wrong, you will always insist that you are right. The simple reason will be that once you followed their advice and found out that when you were right, by their opinion, you were wrong in fact.

So feel out with the Ace, to start, if only to avoid past regrets. Then lead low and see what happens. But that brings up a new problem. What if you find that you have a nice trump hand headed by *two* Aces. Should you begin by leading both? The obvious answer is, you should; but better judgment says, you shouldn't, unless the odds are heavily loaded in your favor and that heans heavily. Your two trump Aces may gather two tricks nicely; but you, yourself, may come a cropper when you find that the opposition is sitting back, ready to bang you with a Ten that your two Aces failed to catch.

Some experts carry it on from there, warning you to beware of the A, A, 10 which they term the *Double-Ace-Ten*. A high bidder is in high glee when he catches this combo in connection with a Sequence, so his trumps run A, A, 10, K, Q, J. Just as with the Double-Ace, there is an urge to lead all three in the hope that the opposing trumps are evenly divided; and if so, you will clear them then and there. But experts point out that the *three-three split* between the opposing hands occurs only about one time out of three, while the odds are about even that they will be divided four-two. In that case, if you have played your Ace, Ace, Ten, there will still be a trump out against you and it is very apt to be the other Ten.

That means that when one opponent plays the Ten later, your other foe can smear it with a counter. So to avoid that problem, players are sometimes advised to hang on to a Double-Ace-Ten and lead the Queen if the Simplified Count is being used; or else lead the Jack, if the Popular Count is being used. The idea here is to force out the opposing Ten, which a lead of your Queen most certainly will do, unless the player holding it has the King with it. If you lead the Jack, his chances of keeping the Ten for a later play are considerably better. But he will generally play it anyway, for fear that when you get the lead back, you will play your Ace-Ace-King and catch his Ten, even if he had four trumps in his hand to start.

But why wait until you get back the lead? What's wrong with the long-established policy of leading the Double-Ace-Ten just because of the danger that your adversaries might gain an extra counter through a smear which may never happen? So leading out your high trumps is still the best bet, but do it in the order Ten, Ace, Ace, instead of starting with the Aces as some players unthinkingly do.

Here's what will happen. If the trumps are equally divided between your adversaries, you will catch the Ten and gain its points as well as avoiding the future smear, thus getting by with the very caper that you were afraid your opponents might manage. But even better, if the opposing trumps are split four-two, as they are half the time, you will have one chance in three that it will be with the player who is holding the two cards. In that case, it will show up on your second lead and you will know immediately which player has the other two trumps.

By making your leads in the order Ten, Ace, Ace, you still have an option if the opposing Ten does not appear on your second lead. Instead of leading your remaining Ace, you can lead your Jack and force out the Ten anyway, even if both the opposing trumps are in one player's hand. He can't afford to hang on to the Ten at this juncture, because it would be his only trump and you would still have an Ace with which to take it.

All this applies to times when a bidder's hand is strong enough in side suits to justify clearing the opposing trumps. If it isn't that good, he shouldn't be leading trumps to start, but should be leading from a side suit.

Playing Against the Bidder

In every deal in Auction Pinochle, the opponents begin to gang up on the successful bidder even before he leads his first card. They do that by studying his meld, thereby learning how to decide where his weaknesses may be. In informal games, the temporary partners sometimes exchange comments regarding the amount of meld showing, but that would not be allowed in more serious play. In fact, it is not necessary as the opponents can see for themselves just how the bidder's meld stands.

The bidder, however, is not entirely at a disadvantage. In the standard Three-Handed game, all players show their melds, so if two decide to gang up on one, they may gain some inklings of each other's hands. But in Auction, only the successful bidder melds, and although this helps his adversaries at the start, they may run into snags as the plays proceed, since neither knows exactly what the other wants. Also, although they have seen the turned-up widow as well as the meld, they can't be sure of just what cards the bidder buried and often he can fool them very neatly on that score.

As a result, the opponents usually follow conventional leads to insure effective play. Chief of these is the Ace-Ten cue. If an opponent holds an Ace and Ten in a side suit, he leads the Ace, which calls for the other opponent to throw on the other Ace if he has it. To beginners, this seems wasteful, as the second Ace might take another trick, but it works well in practice, as the main job is for the opponents to grab all the points they can while the grabbing is good.

Suppose that Lou is the opponent at the dealer's left and that Rick is the opponent at the right. If Lou gives the Ace-Ten cue by leading his Ace and Rick responds by playing the Ace, Lou then leads his Ten, which in turn calls for Rick to play the other Ten if he has it. If Lou leads his Ace and Rick doesn't have the other Ace, he naturally plays a Ten if he has one, as that is the best that he can do. The big angle is that if Rick doesn't play an Ace, Lou knows that the bidder, Bobo, has it, so Lou switches to another suit for his next lead.

If Lou has both Aces of a suit, he can use the same cue quite readily. Rick can't respond with an Ace, but if he has a Ten, he naturally plays it. Either way, Lou proceeds to lead his second Ace and Rick then knows all. If Lou holds Ace-Ace-Ten, his best cue is to lead the Ten, which calls for a Ten from Rick. Lou then proceeds to lead his Aces. If Lou has an Ace, but no other high card in that suit, he should lead from a different suit. He will get his chance to play his Ace later and his partner, Rick, will then know how he stands. The only exception to this rule is when a leader has only an Ace and nothing else in that suit. He should play the Ace to make it good while he can; and his immediate switch to another suit will reveal the situation to his partner.

If Rick has the lead, he can use the same cues, but since Bobo, the bidder, trumps Rick's lead, Lou naturally would not follow the rule of playing an Ace or Ten. Instead, he throws a small card and keeps his big counter to smear one of Rick's leads in another suit. All this raises an important question: From which suit should an opponent lead when he has a fairly equal choice? Generally, the answer is, the suit that will trouble the bidder the most. Forcing the bidder to waste his trumps is the best bet, particularly when he is short on them.

If the bidder's first lead is an Ace from a side suit, it may be a loner and therefore is a good suit to lead back at him. Also, the bidder's meld reveals suits in which the dealer is fairly long, so it is smart for an opponent to lead from another suit. Also, there are times when it is even smarter for an opponent to lead trumps, especially before the bidder is able to establish his side suit.

A very special situation is when an opponent like Lou is strong in the bidder's side suit. Rick, the other opponent, recognizes it. If Rick begins leading trumps, which ordinarily would be nonsensical, in this case he will purposely exhaust Rick's trumps, so that when Lou gets the lead in that big suit, Rick can smear them with high counters instead of trumping them.

VII

TWO-HANDED PINOCHLE

This differs considerably from Auction Pinochle, being practically a game in itself. The melds are the same, but they are progressive and are made singly, during the course of play, which also has its own individual features.

The dealer, A, deals twelve cards to another player, B, and himself, either by threes or fours. He turns up the next card and inserts it partly beneath the pack, which stays face down. The face up card is the trump, and if it is the Dix, Nine, the dealer promptly marks up 10 points as a start towards his score.

The non-dealer, B, leads any card, and A plays any card he wants. He does not have to follow suit or trump at this point. The usual rule holds, however, as to taking the trick. B wins it unless A plays a higher card in that suit, or trumps a lead from an ordinary suit.

Whoever wins the trick can then meld if he has a suitable combination in his hand. Whether or not he melds, he draws the top card from the pack to bring his hand up to 12 cards. The other player does the same and the one who won the trick makes another lead. This continues, play by play, meld by meld, draw by draw.

Melded cards are left face up on the table, but they may be played at any time, instead of playing from the hand. This enables a player to hold onto cards needed for later melds.

If a player has a Dix, he may meld it by sliding it face up under the pack and picking up the trump card showing there. This is done with the second Dix, though in that case, the player merely has to show, it, rather than exchange one Dix for the other. A Dix can be exchanged after a winning trick, and a single meld be put down at the same time. The last card drawn from the pack will be the face up Dix.

At that point, each player gathers up his meld and from there on, the play follows the standard pattern. Whatever the trick-winner leads, the other player must follow suit if he can. Otherwise, he must trump; if out of trumps, he can discard from an odd suit. Any trump lead must be overtrumped.

Scoring the Hands

After the hands have been played out, each player gathers up the tricks that he has taken and goes through them, weeding out counter cards to determine his score.

The counter cards are added up, including 10 for the last trick, and these totals are added to each player's individual meld. The original count is often used in Two-Handed Pinochle, but the players may agree upon some other. The deal then goes to Player B. More hands are played until one player reaches 1000 and becomes the winner.

A running score is kept by one player and by referring to it, a player can usually tell when he has taken enough counters to reach the 100 mark. He can declare out and win the game right there, unless a count proves him to be short, in which case he loses. Or if both players agree, nobody wins if both reach 1000, and the game is extended to 1250, or 1500, etc., until one wins cleanly.

Special Rules for Melding

Special rules apply to the melding in this game. Not only must they be made singly; a meld, to be valid, requires a new card from the hand to complete it.

Thus if a player melds four Kings for 80 and four Queens for 60, he cannot marry any of the Kings and Queens, so 140 is the limit of his meld. His proper course is to meld four Kings, 80; a Royal Marriage, 40; a Plain Marriage, 20; then another Plain Marriage, 20. The can then add the fourth Queen, 60; making a total of 220. Or if he has an odd King or Queen, he can use it to complete the last marriage.

Some players allow the Round House, four Kings and Queens, to be scored as a complete meld of 240, as in the Auction or Three-Handed game. This is fair enough, as a player very rarely has all eight cards available at once.

The following is *always* allowable in the Two-Handed game. If a player makes a Royal Marriage as: **K♠** and **Q♠** for 40 points, he can later add the A, 10, J of trump and score 150 for the sequence. If, however, he melds the A, 10, K, Q, J first, which he may be forced to do when the draw is getting short, he cannot remove the K, Q from the sequence and declare it as a marriage later.

In the original game, a meld of double Pinochle was allowed; namely **J ♦, J ♦, Q♠, Q♠**, for 80 points. By the same token, a player could first meld **J ♦** and **Q♠** for 40 points; then later add the second **J ♦** and **Q♠** and call it double for 80 points more.

Another custom was to regard double Pinochle as a special meld that could only be made *all at once* for a score of 300 points. Today, most players simply count each Pinochle as a 40 meld of its own, so any reversion to the old rules should be mutually understood before the game.

Generally, players are allowed to meld a Dix along with another meld. Thus, a player could meld the **K♣** and **Q♣** for 20 while melding the Nine of trump for 10. But in such a meld, the trump picked up by the Dix cannot be used until later. Also, when a Dix is exchanged for another trump, that trump can definitely be used immediately in a meld. For example: If Hearts are trump, a 9 could be exchanged for a Queen and the Queen could be used to meld a Royal Marriage with a King from the hand. The double transaction scores 50 points.

VIII

A SAMPLE

TWO-HAND DEAL

Here is a complete deal of Two-Handed Pinochle, given play by play from start to finish. The exact status of the hands is shown, along with melds or what remains of them, prior to each draw. Hence, the play of the hands can be followed from the descriptions without any need for a pack of cards.

This is taken from an actual game between two players, Harry and Wally. It is Wally's deal and the hands turn out as follows:

Harry

♠: 10 ♥: 10,K,Q,9,9 ♣: 10,K,Q,9 ♦: A,K

Wally

♠: A,K,K,Q,9 ♥: 10 ♣: Q,J,9 ♦: 10,K,9

Turned up Trump: **J♠**

The play proceeds:

First Trick: Harry leads the **9♥**
Wally takes it with the **10♥**

Wally melds the **K♠, Q♠**, as a Royal Marriage for 40 points and takes up the **J♠** from beneath the pack, putting the Dix in its place for another 10 points.

Score: Harry — 0 Wally — 50

Comment: Wally wanted the **J♠** badly for a possible Trump Sequence and might have trumped the **9♥** with his extra **K♠** to get it. Luckily; he was holding the **10 ♥**, so he didn't have to sacrifice the **K♠**.

Wally draws the **Q♦**. Harry draws the **K♣**.

The hands now stand:

Harry:
♠: 10 ♥: 10,K,Q,9 ♣: 10,K,K,Q,9 ♦: A,K
Wally:
♠: A,K,J ♣: Q,J,9 ♦: 10,K,Q,9
Meld: ♠: K, Q

2nd Trick: Wally leads the **10♦**.
Harry plays the **9♣**.

Wally takes the trick and melds the **K♦, Q♦** as a Plain Marriage for 20 points.

Score: Harry — 0 Wally — 70

Comment: Wally's lead of the **10♦** is debatable. He wanted to meld the Marriage in a hurry and was afraid that Harry might take either the **9♣** or **9♦** if he led one of those. Harry, in turn, should have guessed that Wally was overly eager and might very well have taken the **10♦** with his **A♦**, capturing a valuable counter (the **10♦**). That would have hurt Harry's chances for Four Aces, but with only one Ace in hand, Harry's chances of such a meld were slim, anyway.

Wally draws the **10♣**. Harry draws the **Q♦**.

The hands now stand:

Harry

♠: 10 ♥: 10,K,Q,9 ♣: 10,K,K,Q ♦: A,K,Q

Wally

♠: A,K,J ♣: 10,Q,J,9 ♦: 9

Meld: ♠: K, Q ♦: K, Q

3rd Trick: Wally leads the **9♦**

Harry takes it with the **A♦**.

Harry melds the **K♣**, **Q♣** as a Plain Marriage for 20.

Score: Harry — 20 Wally — 70

Comment: Here, Harry sacrifices the **A♦** and only picks up a non-counter, the **9♦**. But he has sufficient reason for this. Drawing the **Q♦** gave him three Marriages, with chances for Four Kings and Four Queens. He has to get some melds on the board, or he may be stuck with them. He doesn't regret passing up the **10♦**, for if he had taken it with the **A♦**, he wouldn't have drawn the **Q♦**. *Added note:* The reason Harry melds the Club Marriage is because he can play the **K♣** from the board, if need be, because he still has another **K♣** toward Four Kings.

Harry draws the **J♥**. Wally draws the **A♥**.

The hands now stand:

Harry

♠: 10 ♥: 10,K,Q,J,9 ♣: 10,K ♦: K,Q

Meld: ♣: K, Q

Wally

♠: A,K,J ♥: A ♣: 10,Q,J,9

Meld: ♠: K,Q ♦: K,Q

4th Trick: Harry leads the **9♥**

Wally plays the **9♣**

Harry takes the trick and melds the **K♥**, **Q♥** as a Plain Marriage for another 20 points.

Score: Harry — 40 Wally — 70

Comment: Harry's lead of the **9♥** conformed to a sound

policy of leading repeatedly from a long suit. His first lead was the **9♥**; so was his second. His third, the next lead, should be the **J♥**.

Harry draws the **A♦**. Wally draws the **9♦**.

The hands now stand:

Harry

♠: 10 ♥: 10,J ♣: 10,K ♦: A,K,Q

Meld: ♣: K,Q ♥: K,Q

Wally

♠: A,K,J ♥: A ♣: 10,Q,J ♦: 9

Meld: ♠: K,Q ♦: K,Q

5th Trick: Harry leads the **J♥**
Wally plays the **9♦**.

Harry takes the trick and melds the **K♦**, **Q♦** as still another Marriage for 20 points more.

Score: Harry — 60 Wally — 70

Comment: Wally might have thrown the **J♣** and kept the **9♦** for a later lead, since Diamonds is his long suit, but he thinks he might catch Four Jacks. Having nothing to meld, Wally had no reason to take this trick.

Harry draws the **Q♠**. Wally draws the **A♣**.

The hands now stand:

Harry

♠: 10,Q ♥: 10 ♣: 10,K ♦: A

Meld: ♣: K,Q ♥: K,Q ♦: K,Q

Wally

♠: A,K,J ♥: A ♣: A,10,Q,J

Meld: ♠: K,Q ♦: K,Q

6th Trick: Harry leads the **10♥**
Wally plays the **J♣**

Harry takes the trick and melds the **Q♠** alongside the three Queens on the board for a meld of 60 points. (Four Queens).

Score: Harry — 120 Wally — 70

Comment: Harry was anxious to take the trick and make that meld in order to free his Queens for play, as he wants to hold his Kings in hope of drawing the **K♠** for Four Kings. He was lucky, for a trick or two before, Wally would have clobbered Harry's **10♥** with his own **A♥**. But Wally didn't, because he had just drawn the **A♣**, which gave him visions of Four Aces, if he could only pick up the **A♦** to go along with the three he now has. So Wally let the **10♥** win the trick.

Note: Harry can't draw a **K♠**, because Wally has both, though Harry doesn't know it. If Harry should draw the **K♠**, he could meld it with the **Q♠**, as a Royal Marriage for 40 points, but could not score 80 for Four Kings, as a new card would be needed for that meld. Harry, however, has foreseen this and is keeping his extra **K♣** in reserve for just such a situation.

Harry draws the **Q♥**. Wally draws the **J♣**.

The hands now stand:

Harry

♠: 10 ♥: Q ♣: 10,K ♦: A

Meld: ♠: Q ♦: K,Q ♣: K,Q ♥: K,Q

Wally

♠: A,K,J ♥: A ♣: A,10,Q,J

Meld: ♠: K,Q ♦: K,Q

7th Trick: Harry leads the **Q♥** from the board.
Wally plays the **J♣**

Harry takes the trick, but has no meld.

Comment: Harry led the **Q♥** already melded so as to keep the **Q♥** in his hand in case he draws another **K♥**. Wally played the **J♣** because he has given up hope of melding Four Jacks, as his hand is too overloaded with chances for higher melds.

Harry draws the **9♠**. Wally draws the **10♠**.

The hands now stand:

Harry

♠: 10,9 ♥: Q ♣: 10,K ♦: A

Meld: ♦: K,Q, ♣: K,Q ♥: K,Q

Wally

♠: A,10,K,J ♥: A ♣: A,10,Q

Meld: ♠: K,Q, ♦; K,Q

8th Trick: Harry leads the **Q♣**

Wally takes it with the **10♣**

Wally adds the **A♠**, **10♠** and **J♠** to the **K♠**, **Q♠** already on the board, thus melding a Trump Sequence for 150 points.

Score: Harry — 120 Wally — 220

Comment: Since Harry wanted to keep both his Hearts in hope of future melds, he had to open a new suit. He led the **Q♣** rather than the **Q♦** because he had more Clubs than Diamonds and also because Wally had a **K♦** showing on the board and might have used it to take Harry's **Q♦**. A good break for Wally, as he was able to take the trick with the **10♣** without jeopardizing any possible melds. Otherwise, he might have trumped Harry's **Q♣** with his spare **K♠**, because Wally knows he can't use it for another Royal Marriage, as Harry has a **Q♠** showing on the board. But Wally doesn't want Harry to know that he, Wally, has the extra **K♠**. All part of Pinochle strategy.

Wally draws the **10♦**. Harry draws the **J♦**.

The hands now stand:

Harry

♠: 10,9 ♥: Q ♣: 10,K ♦: A,J

Meld: ♦: K,Q ♣: K ♥: K ♠: Q

Wally

♠: K ♥: A ♣: A,Q ♦: 10

Meld: ♠: A,10,K,Q,J ♦: K,Q

9th Trick Wally leads the **10♦**

Harry takes it with the **A♦**.

Harry adds the **J ♦** from his hand to the **Q♠** showing on the board, melding a Pinochle for 40 points. He also melds the **9♠** (Dix) for 10 points.

Score: Harry — 170 Wally — 220

Comment: Wally led the **10♦**, thinking that any of his other cards — with the exception of the spare **K♠** — might be usable in a last moment meld. Harry promptly clobbered the **10♦** with his **A♦**, picking up a valuable counter. Since that was the second **A♦** that Harry played from his hand, Wally knew that he, Wally, now had no chance for Four Aces.

Harry draws the **K♥**. Wally draws the **J♥**.

The hands now stand:

Harry

♠: 10,9 ♥: K,Q ♣: 10,K

Meld: ♦K,Q,J ♣: K ♥: K ♠: Q

Wally

♠: K ♥: A,J ♣: A,Q

Meld: ♠: A,10,K,Q,J ♦: K,Q

10th Trick: Harry leads the **J♦**
Wally plays the **J♥**

Harry takes the trick and melds the **K♥**, **Q♥** from his hand for a Plain Marriage of 20 points.

Score: Harry — 190 Wally — 220

Comment: A double surprise for Wally, who was just shocked by knowing he couldn't get Four Aces and now realizes that he can't expect Four Kings or Four Queens either.

Harry draws the **J♠**. Wally draws the **A♥**.

The hands now stand:

Harry

♠: 10,J,9 ♣: 10,K

Meld: ♦: K,Q ♥: K,K,Q ♣: K ♠: Q

Wally

♠: K ♥: A,A ♣: A,Q

Meld: ♠: A,10,K,Q,J ♦: K,Q

11th Trick: Harry leads the **Q♥**
Wally takes it with the **A♥**
Wally has no meld.

Score: Harry — 190 Wally — 220

Comment: Harry knew that Wally might have drawn a **J♦**. Wally could therefore be hoping to add it to his **Q♠** for a Pinochle. If so, there was really no way for Harry to prevent Wally from melding it. Anything that Harry led, Wally could have taken, even going as high as the **A♠** if Harry had led the **10♠**. So Harry still stayed with his fixed policy of playing the lowest card of his longest suit, the **Q♥**. Wally, though he didn't have the **J♦**, took the **Q♥** with the **A♥**, on the long chance that he might draw the **J♦**, though Wally is almost sure it is in Harry's hand.

Wally draws the **J♦**. Harry draws the **A♠**.

The hands now stand:

Harry

♠: A,10,J,9 ♣: 10,K

Meld: ♥K,K ♣: K ♦: K,Q ♠: Q

Wally

♠: K ♥: A ♣: A,Q ♦: J

Meld: ♠: A,10,K,Q,J ♦: K,Q

12th Trick: Wally leads the **A♠**
Harry plays the **K♥**

Wally takes the trick and puts the **J♦** with the **Q♠**, thus melding a Pinochle for 40 points.

Score: Harry — 190 Wally — 260

Comment: Though Wally was surprised to draw the **J♦**, he recognized that his only chance of cashing in the Pinochle lay in taking the next trick and to do that, he would have to lead the Ace of Trump, so he did. Harry threw on the **K♥**, deciding that it would be trumped later if he didn't play it now.

Wally draws the **A♣**. Harry picks up the **9♠** as the final card. (No score for this as the Dix was melded earlier.)

The players pick up their melded cards and add them to their hands, which now stand as follows:

Harry

♠: A,10,Q,J,9,9 ♥: K ♣: 10,K,K ♦: K,Q

Wally

♠: 10,K,K,Q,J ♥: A ♣: A,A,Q ♦: K,Q,J

From this point on, as stated in the rules, each player must follow suit and if the trump is led, he must overtrump it. Some old-timers go by a bygone rule that a player must *head the trick,* by playing a higher card if a plain suit is led, but this is generally regarded as an obsolete practice which unnecessarily complicates the game. However, if a player is out of a suit, he must trump when it is led, provided he still has a trump in hand.

If both players have kept close track of all the plays and melds to date, as all veteran Two-Handed players do, each will have the advantage of knowing exactly what cards the other has in hand, so the play will often be somewhat automatic. In this case, Wally has a decided edge due to his three Aces and it is his lead, so the play would continue somewhat as follows:

13th Trick: Wally leads the **A♥**
Harry plays the **K♥**
Wally wins **A♥** & **K♥**

14th Trick: Wally leads the **A♣**
Harry plays the **K♣**
Wally wins **A♣** & **K♣**

15th Trick: Wally leads the **A♣**
Harry plays the **K♣**
Wally wins **A♣** & **K♣**

16th Trick: Wally leads the **K♦**
Harry plays the **Q♦**
Wally wins **K♦** & **Q♦**

17th Trick: Wally leads the **J♦**
Harry takes it with the **K♦**
Harry wins the **K♦ & J♦**
18th Trick: Harry leads the **10♣**
Wally plays the **Q♣**
Harry wins the **10♣ & Q♣**
19th Trick: Harry leads the **9♠**
Wally takes it with a **K♠**
Wally wins the **K♠ & 9♠**
·20th Trick: Wally leads the **Q♦**
Harry takes it with the **Q♠**
Harry wins the **Q♠ & Q♦**
21st Trick: Harry leads the **9♠**
Wally takes it with the **K♠**
Wally wins the **K♠ & 9♠**
22nd Trick: Wally leads the **J♠**
Harry takes it with the **10♠**
Harry wins the **10♠ & J♠**
23rd Trick: Harry leads the **J♠**
Wally takes it with the **10♠**
Wally wins the **10♠ & J♠**
24th Trick: Wally leads the **Q♠**
Harry takes it with the **A♠**
Harry wins the **A♠ & Q♠**
Harry also wins the last trick

Now, if we add the tricks just taken to those taken during the earlier play and tabulate each players *take* excluding Nines, we find the following results:

Harry's Take: 3 A's, 4 10's, 1 K, 5 Q's, 7 J's.

Wally's Take: 5 A's, 4 10's, 7 K's, 3 Q's, 1 J.

By the Original Count, which some players still insist on using in Two-Handed Pinochle, this would add as follows:

Harry: A's - 33, 10's - 40, K's - 4; Q's - 15, J's - 14. Total 116.*

Wally: A's - 55, 10's - 40, K's - 28; Q's - 9, J's - 2. Total 134.

*Including 10 points for taking Last Trick.

By the Popular Count, so commonly used today, the points would add up as follows:

Harry: A's - 30, 10's - 40, K's - 5; Q's - 25. Total 110*

Wally: A's - 50, 10's - 40, K's - 35, Q's - 15. Total 140

*Including 10 points for taking Last Trick.

By the Simplified Count, which is less flexible, but easier to figure, both in play and afterward, the result would be:

Harry: A's - 30, 10's - 40, K's - 10. Total 90*

Wally: A's - 50, 10's - 40, K's - 70. Total 160.

*Including 10 points for taking Last Trick.

In each instance, the sum total for the deal is determined by totalling the melds made during the early play and adding the points taken in play throughout the deal. This would be tabulated in the form of a running score, as follows:

Original Count		Popular Count		Simplified Count	
Harry	*Wally*	*Harry*	*Wally*	*Harry*	*Wally*
20	50	20	50	20	50
40	70	40	70	40	70
60	220	60	220	60	220
120	260	120	260	120	260
170	+134	170	+140	170	+160
190	394	190	400	190	420
+116		+110		+ 90	
306		300		280	

Comparison of Results

Considering this as a good representative deal in Two-Handed Pinochle, it is quite apparent that the Popular Count (A = 10, 10 = 10, K = 10, Q = 10) so closely approximates the Original Count (A = 11, 10 = 10, K = 4, Q = 3, J = 2) that the use of the Popular Count should be recommended for modern play. A keen player may give a trifle more attention to his Queens than he would in the old-time game, but the fact that Jacks are disregarded in the modern game generally makes very little difference.

It is always customary to throw off Jacks whenever other cards must be kept for bigger melds. Some examples of this appeared in the sample game just described. Hence, the two-point value for a Jack taken in play is at best a hit-or-miss affair and it would be difficult indeed to picture a Two-Handed game close enough for the final outcome to hinge on a few Jacks taken in play. True, Harry took seven Jacks as opposed to Wally's one, in the sample deal just cited, but Wally offset that by picking up seven Kings to Harry's one. Actually, the Queens are apt to become the deciding factor, whichever count is being used, the Original or the Popular.

The Simplified Count (A = 10, 10 = 10, K = 10) presents a different aspect, as a reference to the sample game will show. There, Harry had to sacrifice Kings because he was overloaded with them; and he was overloaded, because he had been hanging on to Kings, hoping to get Four Kings (**K♠**, **K♥**, **K♣**, **K♦**) for 80 points, because he didn't know that Wally held both Kings of Spades. Meanwhile, Harry had melded Four Queens for 60 points (after taking the Sixth Trick), so he was able to unload Queens.

Now, if it had been the other way about, Harry could have unloaded his Kings by playing them a bit cleverly, cashing in on a few, as he did on the Queens. That explains why the Kings and Queens should be equal as counters (K = 5, Q = 5), both in conformity to the requirements of Modern Pinochle and the demands of the Women's Liberation Movement. So the Popular Count should take precedence in Two-Handed Pinochle as played today. However, dyed-in-the-wool old-timers are still privileged to use the Original Count, cumbersome though it may be.

Two Handed Pinochle is unquestionably one of those games in which experience is by far the best teacher, so the more hands you play, the better will be your understanding of it. However, there are some very interesting angles on both meld and play, which will be covered in the next chapter.

IX

ANGLES

ON MELD

AND PLAY

(In Two-Handed Pinochle)

Since there are 48 cards in a Pinochle pack and each player is dealt 12 cards to start, the chances are close to even that he will receive any specific card he has in mind, since there are two cards of that value in the pack. This can prove highly important where the Dix, or Nine of Trump is concerned, as the following example will show. Assuming Clubs to be trump, the player holds:

♣: A,A,K,Q,J,9

Turned up as trump is the **10♣**.

The player's trump holding alone is shown because it is all that matters in this situation. Assuming that the player is the non-dealer and therefore leads to the first trick, he should obviously lead an Ace of Clubs. Being the highest trump, it will take the trick and he can exchange the Dix (**9♣**) for the **10♣**, scoring 10 for meld. More important, the **10♣** gives him a Trump Sequence which he can meld later for 150 points.

Note: Originally, a Dix could only be melded by itself, but modern practice allows another meld when a Dix is exchanged or shown. So in this case, the player could meld the **K♣**, **Q♣** as a Royal Marriage for 40 points; then meld the Sequence for 150 after he takes another trick.

Now, suppose that the player lacked the **Q♣** as well as the **10♣**, so his holding would stand:

♣: A,A,K,J,9

Turned up as trump: **10♣**

Would that be worth a lead of an **A♣** to make sure of picking up the **10♣**? Most players would say yes, emphatically, because with A, 10, K, J in hand, only a Queen would be needed for both 40 points for a Royal Marriage and 150 for a Sequence later.

Now, take this situation:

♣: A,10,10,K,J,9

Here, a lead of the **A♣** turned up as trump, **Q♣** would be unwise, because the player would have to draw the other **A♣** in order to make his Sequence. It would be better to forget the **Q♣**, because the other **Q♣** could be drawn just as easily — or as luckily — as the other **A♣**. But in this case, the player has a spare **10♣**, so wouldn't it be smart to lead it?

Yes, if the player is willing to take the chance that his adversary does *not* have the other **A♣** in his hand. But if the adversary *does* have it, he is almost certain to guess why the **10♣** was led. So he will take the **10♣** with his **A♣** and if he has the other Dix (**9♣**), he will pick up the **Q♣** himself, spoiling the leader's effort to snare a Sequence.

On that account, some players holding the trumps shown above would prefer to lead something worthless, like a Nine from another suit, hoping the adversary will let it go by, even if he does hold the other Dix. In this case, the leader doesn't tip off the fact that he is strong on trumps, something that may prove to his advantage later. And he still might draw the spare **Q♣**, even if his adversary picks up the one turned up as trump.

Note: If the leader does take the first trick and uses the Dix to pick up the **Q♣**, he can not meld the **K♣**, **Q♣** as a Royal Marriage until he takes another trick. That is because the meld must be completed before the draw is made. A check back on the sample hand will make this quite clear.

Now, suppose the leader simply held:

♣: 10,J,9

Turned up trump: **J♣**

Superficially, it would seem ridiculous to waste the **10♣** in order to pick up another **J♣** when the leader already has one. But figure it from this angle: Having only the Ten and Jack toward a Trump Sequence, the player has very little chance of making one. That means that his adversary may already be well fixed where trumps are concerned, perhaps to the point where the **J♣** would give him a Sequence or something close to it. So by leading the **10♣**, the leader can ruin his adversary's prospects.

Unless the adversary has *both* Aces of Trump, he can't affort to take the **10♣**, or he will ruin his chance for a Sequence. So he is apt to let the leader take the trick, thinking that the other Jack is still in the stock, never suspecting that the leader, far from being after a Sequence of his own, is trying to prevent his adversary from bagging one.

When Melds Become Expendable

Of all *expendable* melds, Four Jacks are usually the first that a player should sacrifice in order to keep something better. If a player is dealt Four Jacks to start, he should meld them as soon as possible in order to cash in his 40 points, because there are only two that he will then have reason to keep: The Jack of Trump and the Jack of Diamonds. If Diamonds happen to be trump, that means that only the Jack of Diamonds needs to be kept.

The Jack of Trump is retained as long as there is a chance to use it as part of a Trump Sequence. The Jack of Diamonds can be teamed with the Queen of Spades for a 40-point Pinochle. Hence, if you have a Queen of Spades as well as Four Jacks, you should meld the **Q♠** with the **J♦** next, as that frees the Jack for play along with other Jacks. If you don't have Four Jacks to start, meld a Pinochle (**J♦**, **Q♠**) if you have one.

How long should three Jacks be kept in hope of drawing a fourth? That question is easily answered: Only as long as they do not cramp the player's meld or play. As a good example. With Clubs as trump, a player holds:

♣: A,10,K,J ♦: A,J ♥: 10,K,Q ♠: 10,K,J

Unfortunately, it doesn't happen to be this player's lead, or he could lead the **10♥** or **10♠**, with a good probability of taking the trick and melding his **K♥**, **Q♥** for a 20-point simple Marriage. Instead, his adversary has the lead and proceeds to lead the **9♦**, which is most embarrassing indeed. The player can't take it with the **J♦**, because he is saving it toward a Pinochle, if he draws the **Q♠**. Nor can he trump it with the **J♣**, because he wants that for a Trump Sequence. He can't sacrifice his Heart Marriage (**K♥**, **Q♥**) and to throw either the **10♥** or **10♠** would be a waste of a good counter. His only way of taking the **9♦** is with the **A♦**, but he now has a fair chance of getting Four Aces, since it is early in the deal. He is also after Four Kings, so he can't throw the **K♠**.

So the player gives up any idea of Four Jacks and throws the **J♣** on his opponent's lead of the **9♦**. That relieves the situation greatly, because the player may draw another card that he can throw away; and better still, if the adversary leads a low Heart of Spades next, the player can hit it with one of his Tens and promptly meld his Heart Marriage.

That brings up the question of Four Queens and Four Kings. Like Four Jacks, either of those combinations should be melded as soon as possible. But they not only count more than Jacks, they are usable in Marriages as well, so it is bad to sacrifice them. In the example just shown, the player has a Marriage already, with three cards toward a meld of Four Kings. Even if he should draw a **K♦**, filling his Four Kings, he should meld the Marriage (**K♥**, **Q♥**) first, because unless he draws another Queen quite soon, he will have to give up hopes of Four Queens, just as he did with Four Jacks. That would make the **Q♥** expendable, once it has been melded with the **K♥** as a Marriage.

Whether he plays the **Q♥** or not, the player should use each new Queen toward a Marriage with one of his Kings, but here is another word of caution. After completing a third Marriage, he should draw both his fourth King and his fourth Queen before he has a chance to meld his Four Kings, he should still meld the Four Kings and not the fourth Marriage, as he can not use the same card toward both. The same rule would apply with the Four Queens; they should be melded when he lays down the fourth Queen, instead of declaring the fourth Marriage. The layout could then look like this:

	Plain Marriage	*Royal Marriage*	*Plain Marriage*	*Plain Marriage*	
Kings	**K♥**	**K♣**	**K♦**	**K♠**	*80 pts.*
Queens	**Q♥**	**Q♣**	**Q♦**	**Q♠**	*60 pts.*
	20 pts.	*40 pts.*	*20 pts.*	XX	

The melder's final total is 220 instead of 240, so he loses a mere 20 points, by not melding the final Marriage. But if he had declared it instead of the Four Queens, his total would have been reduced to 180; and if he had declared it earlier instead of the Four Kings, he would have lost both the Four Kings and the Four Queens, reducing his final total to 100.

Any of these lost melds can be regained by adding an extra King or Queen — or both — to the layout, provided the melder has such a card or cards in his hand. But that takes time, so the best way is to get the Kings and Queens on the board and not worry about the 20 points for the last Marriage.

Four Aces is one of the biggest melds in the pack and generally the least worrysome if the player gets it before the drawing process is too far along. If he gets his Aces early, the best advice is to hold them back and surprise your opponent with them later. If you have an odd Ace with them, all the better, for your adversary may be holding three of his own and therefore be sacrificing other melds in hope of drawing a fourth Ace that he can't possibly get. Of course, if your own hand becomes cramped with too many prospective melds, you should put your Four Aces on the board, because once they are melded you can use the non-trump Aces to take tricks, particularly when your foe leads a Ten.

If you hold two non-trump Aces of the same suit — as **A♦**, **A♦** — you can use one early to take a needed trick, but that tells your foe that he can't get Four Aces and thus enables him to use any Aces of his own toward taking important tricks. But this piece of advice has a neat reverse twist. If all you have is a lone Ace, preferably non-trump, your chances of drawing the other three becomes virtually nil, unless you draw one or two very soon. So as the draw progresses, it is smart to use the lone Ace to win a trick enabling you to make an important meld like Four Kings or Four Queens, or even Four Jacks which you might otherwise have to sacrifice.

In that case, your opponent, unless he already has Four Aces himself, may logically suppose that you have played a duplicate Ace through necessity or unthinkingly and therefore he has no chance of making Four Aces. Working from that supposition, he may begin using his Aces as trick-takers and his chagrin will be great indeed if he suddenly draws the duplicate of the Ace you played and finds he could have made his Four Aces after all.

Never regret a timely play if it looks unfortunate later, as that is simply part of the game and often is not as bad a mistake as it seems and in fact may not be a mistake at all. Here is an actual illustration:

With only a few more draws to come, a player drew a **J ♦** to go with a **Q ♠** that he had already melded. His opponent led a **10 ♦** and the player had a chance to take it with an **A ♦**. The trouble was, he also held the **A♣** and the **A♥**, so he only needed the **A♠** for Four Aces. But the Pinochle was sure; the Four Aces weren't. So instead of throwing an odd Nine on to his opponent's **10 ♦**, he smacked it with the **A ♦**, capturing a 10-pointer and melding his **J ♦** with the **Q♠** for 40 more. But his joy turned to grief when the next card he drew from the pack proved to be the **A♠** that he wanted for Four Aces.

A week later, this player was still griping over how he had done himself out of a *Hundred Ace* meld, when a friend commented, "Why, if you had let that trick go, you couldn't have gotten the fourth Ace anyway, because it wouldn't have been your turn to draw!" That was the absolute truth, so whenever you have a similar disappointment, don't gripe. Think it over and you, too, may find it didn't really matter.

One last note: After melding a card, you sometimes either have a duplicate, or happen to draw one. If you decide to play one of those cards, play the one you already melded; not the one you have in your hand. Sometimes the card in hand may be usable in a new meld later; but even if that can't happen, it's still better to play from the board, because you won't be giving your keen-eyed rival any information regarding your hand. That's good Pinochle, especially in the Two-Handed game.

X

PINOCHLE FOR FOUR PLAYERS

When four or more players participate in a game of Pinochle, partnership play is usually in order. This is not always the case. In the old days, four players often played a game of straight Pinochle, each on his own, and that game can still be played today. Each is dealt twelve cards, with the final card turned up as trump. Rules then followed the original Three-Handed game. That is:

If the dealer turns up the Nine of Trumps, he is credited with 10 points for a Dix and takes the card up into his hand. If he turns up another value, say the Jack of Clubs, the first player on the dealer's left who holds a Nine of Clubs exchanges it for the Jack and is credited with 10 points for the Dix. The dealer takes up the Nine of Clubs, but gets no credit for it.

Each player then melds whatever he can and each is so

credited on the score sheet. Any player holding the other **9♣** can meld it as a 10-point Dix, but the dealer is stuck with the one he picked up, because another player already melded it. Actually, he is not too badly stuck, because he at least gains a trump card for his hand, which may prove a help in the long run.

After the meld, play begins from the dealer's left and it proceeds just as in Three-Handed Pinochle, except that there are four players instead of three. Deal follows deal and whoever reaches 1,000 first becomes the winner. So it sounds like a good, exciting game, which it sometimes is, but often isn't. There are times when it may be good, but not exciting; and in the opinion of some Pinochle enthusiasts a game that isn't exciting can't be good.

With four individual players, each receives less cards than usual, hence the melds are proportionately smaller. The counters are divided among four players instead of only three. Both of these factors tend to slow the game, with the result that there are frequent hands in which a player is lucky if he registers 100 points. Thus a game can become a snail's race, in which one player merely manages to outcrawl the others, unless somebody is lucky enough to rack up a big meld somewhere along the line. In that case, the others have so much trouble catching up that the outcome is practically a foregone conclusion.

In contrast to that rather drab outlook, Four-Handed Pinochle can become a keen contest indeed when partnership play is introduced. Here, the players seated opposite become partners, combining their melds and counters, which combines the keen competition of the Two-Handed game with the fast play of Three-Handed Pinochle, with other elements as well. For convenience as well as clarity, the varied forms of Partnership Pinochle will therefore be described in the order of their development.

Standard Partnership Pinochle

Each player is dealt twelve cards, preferably by threes, but sometimes by fours and the final card is turned up for trump, as already described. The players seated opposite are partners, so each takes special note of the other's meld — and sometimes lack of meld — since this has a great bearing on the coming play. Take a game with four players: Albert, Barney, Conrad, and Duncan, the dealer. Albert and Conrad, being seated opposite, are partners; so are Barney and Duncan.

Each melds as usual and the partners add their totals toward the team's meld. This, however, does not mean that they can interchange or combine their melds. Those must be kept strictly separate, so that the totals of the individual melds are added. Thus, if Albert should meld **K♠**, **Q♠** for a 20-point Marriage; and Conrad should meld **J♦**, **J♣**, **J♥**, **J♠** for a 40-point Four Jacks, it would be nice indeed if they could lay those melds together and collect 40 points for a Pinochle (**J♦**, **Q♠**). But such is not allowable. Albert's meld would stay at 20, Conrad's at 40, making a total of 60 for the team.

If, in the same deal, Barney melded **K♠**, **Q♠** and **K♦**, **Q♦**; while Duncan melded **K♣**, **Q♣** and **K♥**, **Q♥**, with Clubs as trump, Barney melds 40 for a Royal Marriage and 20 for a Plain Marriage, making 60, while Duncan melds two Plain Marriages for 40, giving them a team meld of 100. But if they could have interchanged their melds, they would have garnered 80 more for Four Kings and 60 more for Four Queens, boosting a grand total to 240, since the whole setup would constitute a Round House.

In play, the tricks are simply stacked together, as in many other types of trump games. One player usually takes care of that for his team and later runs through their combined tricks to total the counters they have taken. The fact that the team's tricks are stacked up together does not alter the order of the play. Whoever takes a trick leads to the next and this rule is followed throughout, just as if the players were operating individually.

Since there are only two teams, scores pile up twice as fast as they would with four individual players and if one team suddenly forges ahead, a lucky meld by one of the opposing players can bring the rival team back into the game, particularly if they can take a big quota of counters as well. But there, another factor enters: team play. This was covered to a degree in the Three-Handed game, in cases where two players have to act as temporary partners in order to waylay an opponent who is on the verge of winning a game or a big bid. But in partnership play, it takes on a larger status.

There, each team is trying to offset the other. If one player is strong on trumps and knows that his partner has a long suit, he must first clear the trumps, then find a way to get the lead into his partner's hand. Otherwise, he will be forced to trump his partner's sure tricks in that long suit. If a player has a long suit, but is short on trumps, he will also want to get the trumps out to make his long suit good. Therefore, in a simple partnership play, the first step is to find out where the trumps are and act accordingly.

That is easy when a player holds high trumps, heading a long suit. Suppose Spades are trump and Albert, the lead-off, holds ♠: A, A, 10, J, 9. He leads the **10♠**, Barney puts on a **10♠**, Conrad, a **K♠** and Duncan a **J♠**. Albert immediately knows this: He had five Spades to start. His partner, Conrad, had melded the Dix (**9♠**). Duncan, the dealer, had melded a Pinochle (**Q♠**, **J♦**). Now, why should Barney throw the valuable **10♠** on Albert's sure-win lead? Obviously, because the **10♠** was the only trump that Barney held.

With four Spades still in Albert's hand (A, A, J, 9) and four already played (10, 10, K, J) that left four divided between Conrad and Duncan. Those four consisted of the **K♠**, **Q♠**, **Q♠**, **9♠**. Albert knows that Conrad has the **9♠**, because Conrad melded it; also that Duncan has a **Q♠**, because Duncan melded a **Q♠** and **J ♦** for a Pinochle. What Albert wants to know now is whether one player holds three of those trumps as opposed to the other's one; and also which player holds the missing King. This is important, because if Duncan, the opposing player, holds three trumps headed by the **K♠**, that card could become a trick taker.

From the meld and the trick just played, Albert learns all. First, Duncan can't have the **K♠**, because if he did have it, he would have melded it for a Royal Marriage with the **Q♠** that he showed when he melded his Pinochle. But there is still another **Q♠** that Albert is anxious to locate, for if Conrad has it, he will be holding three trumps against Duncan's one. However, further analysis on Albert's part proves that Conrad can't have the extra **Q♠**, because if he did have it, he would have melded it with the **K♠** that he put on the first trick.

So the four trumps are obviously an even split, with Conrad holding the **K♠**, **9♠**, while Duncan has the **Q♠**, **Q♠**. This means that if Albert has strong enough support in other suits, he could clear the trump with his two Aces and still have trumps that could be used to regain the lead.

For example, say that Albert's full hand stood:

♠: A,A,10,J,9 ♥: 10,10,K,J ♣: A ♦: A,J

Albert's lead of the **10♠** is the conventional way of telling his partner that he has both Aces over the Ten. The opponents learn that, too, but it doesn't matter. After clearing trump with his two Aces, Albert would lead the **A♣**, as it is his only Club and he can't risk being caught with it after he has given up the lead. He can hold the **A ♦**, because he has the **J ♦** with it, and it can be used for re-entry. His immediate situation involves the Hearts. If his opponents hold both Aces, he will have to lose his King and Jack in order to make good his Tens.

So he leads the **K♥**, forcing an **A♥**. If the opponents take the next trick with the other **A♥**, he throws the **J♥** and they can only take one more trick with an **A♦**, if they have it. If they should lead the **A♣**, Albert would have to trump it, then lead the **J♥** to bring out the other **A♥**. If an opponent also has an **A♦** and leads it, Albert simply throws on the **J♦** and is sitting pretty. If an oppoent leads a Club, he takes it with his last trump; he can take a Heart with a **10♥**; and a Diamond with his **A♦**. The remaining tricks will all be his.

All this can be done without any aid from Conrad, who is simply Albert's silent partner, if the play proceeds as described. But if Conrad holds either an **A♥** or the other **A♦**, not only will they be sure of nine tricks, they should take a tenth. Nevertheless, this hand, if played as described, can give Albert trouble if Conrad has nothing to offer besides the three trumps he had at the start (**K♠**, **K♠**, **9♠**). If the opponents, guessing that Albert is out of Clubs, keep playing that suit each time they get the lead, forcing him to use up his trumps before he can draw out the three Aces that are against him, they may bag a few of Albert's anticipated counters and Last Trick as well.

This case has been detailed in order to emphasize an important phase of Partnership Pinochle which is too often overlooked. Even though a hand appears to be dominant in trumps, it is poor policy to waste trump leads by using two of your team's trumps to take one trump from a single adversary. If Barney and Duncan had been holding two trumps each after the first trick, with Conrad out of trumps, clearing the trumps with the Aces would have been Albert's best bet, since he would have been getting two for one. But as it actually stood, with Conrad and Duncan holding two trumps each and Barney entirely out, Albert was only getting one for two.

Albert's proper course, therefore, was to lead his **10♠** to the first trick as he did; then, finding that Barney had only the lone **10♠**, Albert could have led his **A♣** — as he did — and then the **K♥**, to open that suit. If Albert's partner, Conrad, had failed to provide any help, Albert would have known the truth then and there, which would have enabled him to change his plan of play accordingly, while he still has two Aces of Trump in hand. Also, he could count on some help from Conrad, for his partner still had two trumps, the **K♠** and **9♠**, that might prove useful.

Much more could be said along this line, but the best way to develop skill in Partnership Pinochle is through actual play. The standard Four-Handed game, with play beginning at the dealer's left, as just described, is in some ways the best for this purpose, because it brings up odd problems that often take the player unaware, particularly when he lacks some of the clues that occur in the bidding game which will be described later.

Actually, partners have to provide or concoct clues of their own, which applies to the bidding game as well. In the deal just outlined, Albert's early lead of the **A♣** was a tipoff to Conrad that if he took the next trick (Albert's lead of the **K♥**), he was not to come back with a Club, as Albert might have to trump it, and wouldn't want to do so that early. The Heart lead, however, should tell Conrad that Albert was trying to force out the Aces and that if Albert took the trick with an **A♥**, he should lead back in that suit.

A low lead in a suit, in contrast to an Ace, therefore invites a return lead, for one reason or another. Suppose that on the next deal, Barney, the opener, should find himself a lot better off on this occasion, having two cards of the trump suit, Hearts, the **10♥** and **J♥**. All the rest of his cards are Spades and Clubs, of fair possibilities except for one lone Diamond, the **Q♦**.

Now, Barney would like to get into Clubs or Spades, but one thing worries him. If the other team starts leading trumps, with both Aces, they will catch Barney's **10 ♥** on the second trick they lead.

So Barney leads the **Q ♦**. Conrad plays a **K ♦**, Duncan, who has an **A ♦**, takes the trick, with Albert throwing on a **9 ♦**. Now, Duncan has picked up Barney's cue; he knows that Barney wants the Diamond lead returned, but he thinks that Barney may be wanting to force out the other **A ♦** in order to make good a **10 ♦**. The same idea strikes Albert, who happens to be holding both an **A ♦** and a **10 ♦**. So when Duncan leads back with a **9 ♦**. Albert slaps on the **10 ♦**, intending to lead his **A ♦** next. But Barney, instead of playing a low Diamond, trumps the trick with the **10 ♥**. Conrad, playing last, is forced to deliver the **10 ♦**, which the others thought Barney had, because Conrad only held two Diamonds, the **K ♦** and **10 ♦**.

So Barney cashed his inadequately protected **10 ♥** and took two Diamond counters from the opposing team, counters that they might have won if they had gained the trump lead early enough to bag Barney's **10 ♥**, because they each held an **A ♥**.

Unlike Three-Handed Pinochle, where each player is dealt 16 cards and may quite frequently hold a well-balanced hand of three to five cards in each suit, Partnership Pinochle, with its 12 cards to each player, abounds in one- and two-card suits. Not only are there less cards for each player, there is one more player, which increases the number of short suits. If a player has an Ace in a three-or-four card suit, he should make it his first lead in that suit, unless trumps have already been cleared. If he leads another card first, thinking that he can cash the Ace later, he is apt to find to his discomfort that he can't. Somebody is apt to trump it just that quick.

Similarly, it's no use to play low on a trick that you could take with an Ace. You may be trying to fool the opposition, only to fool yourself instead. A *doubleton,* consisting of an Ace and just one other card of that suit, can be retained as a *sleeper* provided the two cards are retained intact, until the time comes to lead from that suit or somebody leads from the suit itself. Then, leading the Ace becomes a must and the same applies to playing it on a trick that it can take. If you lead low, an adversary may take low; then lead his Ace to trap yours. Or if you let the chance slide by, thinking somebody else will be forced to use his Ace, he may catch you with the same caper.

Normally, when a player leads an Ace, his partner should play a counter on it. This can be a King or Queen with the Popular Count (either being worth 5 points) or a King with the Simplified Count (10). Often a player should play a Ten instead, when using the Popular Count; and if he only has a Ten as a counter, he should always play it unless he is positive that it will take a sure trick later. There is one exception to this rule, however, which serves as a valuable clue.

If a player leads an Ace and his partner has the other Ace, along with a counter and a lower card — for example, ♥: A, K, 9 — he should play the low card. This informs the leader that his partner has the other Ace and invites a repeat lead of that same suit. This occasionally works nicely despite itself. Suppose that Albert leads the Ace of another suit, say the **A♣**, when Spades are trump. Barney, the second player, puts on the **Q♣**. Conrad, Albert's partner, adds the **9♣** and Duncan, Barney's partner, the **J♣**. Albert wins the trick.

Now, Albert also has the **10♣**, his only remaining Club. So he leads the **10♣** in response to Conrad's "cue" of a low card. Confident that Conrad has the other Ace, Albert stares in amzement when Barney triumphantly plays the Ace. But the amazement fades to understanding when Conrad plays the **J♠** — *a trump card* — and Duncan is forced to add another counter in the form of a **K♣**, having nothing else.

So the Albert-Conrad team wins the trick, with the cue working perfectly, because Conrad hadn't anything to play except a low card to tell his partner, "You know me, Al. I don't have the Ace, but I can trump the trick, which is better."

Nice cues can be introduced as an off-beat. Take another deal where Duncan, with a strong trump hand headed by A, A, 10, 10, K of Diamonds, is clearing out the opposition, our old friends Albert and Conrad. Duncan has just one worry. He hasn't any Aces in the other suits. Once he has cleared the trump, he would like to lead a suit which is suitable to Barney. But how can he find that suit?

Easy does it. Leave it to Barney. As Duncan leads his Diamonds, winning trump by trump, Barney runs out of trumps. So, naturally, he throws a counter from a side suit. The play runs:

Duncan: **A♦** Albert: **9♦** Barney: **Q♦** Conrad: **9♦**
Duncan: **A♦** Albert: **J♦** Barney: **K♠** Conrad: **J♦**
Duncan: **10♦** Albert: **K♦** Barney: **9♠** Conrad: **Q♦**

Barney has spelled out the message. If you didn't get it, Duncan did, so study it more closely. While Albert and Conrad were harboring their diminishing trumps, Barney, already diminished after the first trick, gave Duncan a **K♠**. That was a nice counter, a King, but Barney might have thrown a Ten in another suit. However, Barney could be telling Duncan just what Duncan wants to know: That Barney would like Duncan to lead a Spade, because Barney might take a trick in that suit, naturally with an Ace of Spades.

Now, on the next trick, Duncan expected Barney to come up with something like **K♣**, **Q♣**, or even a **J♣**, to say, "I have an **A♣**, too." Only, Barney didn't. He supplied a feeble little **9♠**, which wasn't even a counter, but said the same thing that **K♠** said: "I have an Ace of Spades." Funny thing, that

Barney would be saying it twice. Except that Pinochle is a funny game, in which all the cards are duplicated, making two of each.

It happened that Duncan had just two Spades, a **Q♠** and a **9♠**, which he hadn't felt were helpful to his hand. Now, he liked them. He fed the **9♠** to his partner, Barney, who took it with the **A♠** and promptly led back the other **A♠** to take Duncan's **Q♠**. Barney's message was now quite plain. Each Spade that he had discarded stood for an Ace. The fact that his second discard was a worthless Nine simply emphasized the situation.

XI

AUCTION PINOCHLE WITH PARTNERS

This is a popular outgrowth of Partnership Pinochle that has largely superseded the original game. However, melding, playing and scoring follow the original pattern, so the phases covered in the previous chapter apply to the various forms that follow. The big difference is that instead of turning up a card to designate the trump for that deal, the players, beginning at the dealer's left, bid for the privilege of naming trump, which goes to the highest bidder, who is sometimes given the privilege of leading to the first trick, which can prove highly vital in advanced forms of the game. His partner, of course, is committed to go along with him, just as in the basic game, their melds and counters being scored as a team.

The biggest advantage in naming trump comes when a player is dealt a Sequence (A, 10, K, Q, J) in any suit, as he can name that suit as trump instead of hoping that a right card will turn up. Whatever the amount bid, the team must make that many points or more — through meld and play — in order to score the total. If the team falls short of that mark, the amount of the bid is deducted from its score. The non-bidding team scores its meld and count in either case.

The game is usually put at the standard figure of 1,000 points and if the result is very close, the bidding team has a decided advantage during the final deal, as the bidding team's points are always counted first, so if it just barely tops the 1,000 mark, the bidders win, no matter how far over the opposing team's score may go.

As a guide to successful bidding, a player should first evaluate his hand, allowing for his partner's as well. This differs considerably from the appraisal used in the Three-Handed bidding game, where everything is on an individual basis. As a pattern for Partnership play, note this hand:

♠: A,Q,9 ♥: A,Q,9 ♣: 10,K,J ♦: 10,K,J

This is about as close to a balance as can be dealt and if all four hands were like it with suits so arranged that each team would counteract the other where trumps were concerned, each player would normally take three tricks, which would include 60 points in counters out of the 240 total. That would mean a score of 130 for the team lucky enough to take the last trick, against 120 for the opponents.

Since each Ace should normally take two tricks, with a Ten having an even chance of a capture, each Ace can be valued at

20 points in play, with a Ten being valued at 10 points. But once a player is dealt more than his quota of three trumps, new trick takers are added to his hand; and those, too, can be rated in terms of counters. To take the ultimate example, suppose a player is dealt *all twelve trumps,* giving him this fabulous hand:

♠: A,A,10,10,K,K,Q,Q,J,J,9,9

This hand rates 20 for each Ace and 10 for each Ten, giving it an initial count of 60 points. But it is sure to take 240 counters in play (excluding 10 for Last Trick, which simply falls with the rest). That means 60 for the Aces and Tens, plus 180 for all trumps over three, or nine extra trumps. Divide 180 by nine and each additional trump gains a 20-point rating. Based on that formula, it is a rather simple matter to appraise the playing value of hands generally:

Take this one:

♥: A,10,K,Q,J ♠: K,Q ♦: A,K,K,J,J

By gaining the bid, the player holding this hand named Hearts as trump, giving him a meld of 150 for a Sequence, 20 for a Plain Marriage (in Spades), 40 for a Pinochle (**Q♠, J♦**) for a total of 210. But he could hardly have expected to gain the bid that cheaply. The question is, how much higher could he bid on prospects of counters to be taken in play?

Added up, his point gives two Aces for 40, a Ten, bringing it to 50 and two extra trumps, upping it to 90. Total value: 210 + 90 = 300. But that goes for the player's hand alone. There are 150 points in counters (not including the Last Trick) that should be taken by the other three players. One of those players is the bidder's partner. If he takes his share of 50 points, that will give the bidder a total of 350, as an estimated bid.

That might be shaving it a bit too close, if the partner's help should prove highly erratic; but a bidder might well risk it, figuring that if his partner's hand lacked playing strength, it would probably come up with a meld such as a Plain Marriage and a Dix, which would make up the needed difference.

This method of evaluation is applicable to all forms of Partnership Pinochle in which bidding is involved. So the next step is to describe the games in the order of their development:

Single Bid Partnership

Each player beginning at the dealer's left, either passes or makes a required minimum bid. Originally, the minimum was 100 and when played on that basis, the first bidder can use his bid to inform his partner how much meld he has. Suppose that Albert, the first bidder, has a hand devoid of Aces, but replete with Jacks and Nines, a dud where playing value is concerned. But it does contain a meld of Four Jacks for 40 points and a Marriage in Diamonds for 20. Albert could bid 160, practically saying that he has a meld of 60, but nothing else. That's for the benefit of Conrad, Albert's partner.

Barney, the second bidder, has a Pinochle (**Q♠, J♦**) good for 40 points, but no other meld. However, he has three Aces, which could be helpful to his partner, Duncan, in play. So Barney bids 170. Coming right after Albert's 160, this indicates that Barney has something better than 160, though it isn't all meld. From there on, Conrad and Duncan can weigh their respective hands, incorporate the information each received from his partner and bid accordingly.

To toughen the bidding process, a rule was introduced requiring each player to make a minimum bid of 200, or else pass. Now to be worth 200, a hand would need three Aces, two Tens, five cards in a suit good enough for trump and a meld of 80 points. As a result, various conventions were introduced, such as a bid of 200 to signify a good supporting hand for whatever bid the original bidder's partner might make. A bid of 240 or 260 (whichever is agreed upon beforehand) can be used by a player holding a meld of Four Aces, which are worth 100 points in meld and 80 in play, enough to encourage a partner to bid much higher. A bid of 250 or 270 can mean that the bidder has a Sequence and therefore wants to keep the bid so he can name his trump. Often, the bidder can go much higher with such a hand; and a good angle here is to reserve *odd numbers* for such a bid, as 310, 350, etc., telling the partner to let it ride, unless he happens to have a Sequence of his own, with more trimmings to go with it.

From such conventions, various games have been developed, one of the most popular being:

Firehouse Pinochle

This game calls for the team's first bidder to meet specific requirements at certain bidding levels. The minimum, 200 signifies a better than average playing hand with a meld of anything up to 60 points. A bid at the 250 level definitely means that the bidder holds Four Aces. The 300 level stands for a Sequence, warning the partner to let the bidder keep it, unless the partner has a Sequence of his own.

Along with those sound announcements are further bits of valuable data indicated by setting the bid a notch or so higher. A 10-point lift means that the hand has a good, long suit, that the bidder could use for trump if his partner lets him keep the bid. That goes for 210 or 260. Bidding 20 points above basic level, as 220 or 270, shows a meld of more than 60, up to 120. By combining such information, a bid of 230 or 280 means both extra playing strength and extra meld. Another 10 points for an initial meld of 240 or 290 means a still bigger meld of 120 to 180 or even better.

These are all *initial* bids, made by the first two players to the dealer's left, so that their respective partners can take it or leave it as they choose. The brackets are much the same in the information given, the big difference being that in the higher bracket, 250 to 290, it is understood that everything is in addition to the Four Aces in the bidder's hand. From 300 up, there are no sidelights, as the bidder wants the bid for himself and goes as high as seems safe, with the understanding that his partner is entitled to bid higher if positive he can do better.

If nobody bids, as can happen when hands are all rather mediocre, the dealer must take the bid at 200. As a result, the player at his left often passes, hoping to see the dealer saddled with a losing hand. The second player, being the dealer's partner, is more sympathetic and is apt to bid 200 if he feels his hand has any possibilities. Of course, if the dealer has a good hand, none of that bothers him. Having the final say, he doesn't have to worry about anybody overbidding him.

However, on that account, bonus scores for making bids have become a common feature of Firehouse Pinochle. They will be found in the section on *Bonus Scores*.

Partnership with Unrestricted Auction

Commonly termed simply "Partnership Auction," this is the standard Partnership game, but with no restrictions whatever as to the bidding, other than the fact that once a player has passed, he is out of the bidding. Actually, a player holding a Marriage as his only meld could open the bidding with 20 if he wanted; but in many games, a bidder will start at 100 to speed the auction. In fact, 100 is a conventional bid, as it can be interpreted as *zero*, meaning that the bidder has no meld, something his partner should know.

The only two conventional bids needed are the cue for Four Aces, which can be set at both 240 and 260, each an *even total;* and the cue for a Sequence, which can be set at 250, an *odd total,* which can be jumped to 270 or 290, if needed. The idea is simply this: A player holding Four Aces bids 240, to tell his partner that he has that important meld. But suppose that before he has a chance to do so, an opponent bids 250, telling *his* partner that *he* has a Sequence. The man with the Four Aces still wants to get his message through to his partner, so since he can't bid 240, he does it by bidding 260. It's that simple.

With Unrestricted Auction, a team can agree to this: When one player makes a solid bid, his partner can respond by adding his own meld toward a higher bid. So the original bidder can let it go at that, or take over the bid himself, by bidding one point higher. That can go back and forth as long as necessary, particularly if the other team gets into the act and tries to do the same. Then, the important thing is not to overdo it. If the other team is really anxious to take the bid for themselves, let them have it. But make sure that it has gone so high that if they lose, they will regret it.

That's Auction Partnership with Unrestricted Bidding.

Unrestricted Auction with a Widow

If you think that you have heard everything, you haven't. Bidding can go high indeed in Unrestricted Auction, but when a widow is introduced into the game, it becomes more than Unrestricted. It becomes Unlimited.

To allow for the widow, the hands are reduced from twelve cards to eleven. A neat way of doing this is to deal three cards to each player, laying the next card aside for the widow. Do that three times; then deal a round of two cards each and you will have another extra card for the widow. That gives each player eleven cards instead of twelve, with a four-card widow that is to become the property of the highest bidder.

Bidding is the same as in Unrestrtricted Auction, but with this added factor: Often, a player will have a hand that depends on one or more fills from the widow, as discussed in detail under the head of Three-Handed Auction. If playing on his own, a bidder wouldn't have to advertise that fact; indeed, he might not want to do so. But in the partnership game, he has to tell his partner in order to avoid conflicts in their bidding. That can be managed quite simply by using the odd total bid to mean that the bidder needs the widow in order to complete his meld.

Actually, the bidder is in the same situation as when he holds a Sequence and wants to gain the bid in order to make trump, as otherwise, his hand can't meet the requirements of the bid. In that case, the convention of bidding 250 is the tipoff, so in this case, *any other odd bid* — such as 230 or 290 or higher — can mean that the bidder wants the widow and it is up to his partner to decide whether to let him take it or not.

Bidding a lower figure, as 230, is the best approach, because the bidder's partner might have a full-fledged Sequence in his hand and would therefore be anxious to announce it by bidding the customary 250. However, if the bidding has gone too far for that, the player holding the Sequence can simply bid the next highest odd total to prove that his bid is solid.

For example: The first bidder, Albert, has Four Aces and bids 240. Barney, the next bidder, has a hand that will be worth 350 if he can fill it from the widow. He can't bid 250, for then Barney's partner, Duncan, will think that Barney has a Sequence already in hand. So Barney bids 270, meaning that he wants the widow. Conrad, Albert's partner, passes. Now it happens that Duncan already has a Sequence, but can't give the cue bid of 250, so he bids 290, the next *odd total* above Barney's 270.

What if Duncan has a hand that also depends on the widow and might be a better bet than Barney's? How could he indicate that? Very simply, by jumping the bid to a higher odd total, as 310 instead of 290, or to the limit that he intends to bid, such as 370. If Barney wants to go beyond that, he will be welcome to do so. The main thing is that each partner knows what the other is after and can therefore choose whatever course seems best.

Chances of getting a fill from the widow are better in Partnership Pinochle than in Three-Handed Auction, because there are four cards in the widow, instead of only three. Take this hand as an example:

♠: A,10,Q,J ♦: A,10,K,J ♣: A,A,J ♥: J

The player already has a meld of 40 for Four Jacks, 40 for a Pinochle, making a total meld of 80. The hand, as it stands, has a playing value of 120 and the partner's hand should be good for 50 points more. That comes to 250. There are three possible fills from the widow. The **A ♥** will produce Four Aces, worth 100 in meld, 20 in play, for 370. The next fill the **K ♠**, will produce 150 for a Sequence and 20 for adding another trump in Spades, a prospect of 420. The third possible fill, the **Q ♦**, will do the same in Diamonds, another prospective 420.

Naturally, the bidder won't want to stretch his hopes too far. He might like to play it quite safely by stopping at 350, or even 410. That is up to him to decide. The main thing is that with three possible fills, the chances of catching one of the needed cards is about 2 out of 3 in the bidder's favor.

A hand with two possible fills is much more common and would give the bidder slightly better than an even chance of making it, because of those four cards in the widow. Coming

Summary of Partnership Auction

Introduction of conventional bids can be helpful to all forms of Partnership Auction, provided they are kept within reasonable bounds. With single bids, very few are needed; with a continuous auction, more are needed, but they must be kept simple, otherwise they can defeat their own purpose. When Auction with a widow is introduced, this becomes all the more important.

Most essential is the matter of keeping the bidding open. Suppose that Albert opens with 180, indicating a meld of 80 points. The next bidder, Barney, makes a bid of 280. Following that, Albert's partner, Conrad, goes to 290, indicating that he would like to take the bid with something above that figure; or, in Auction with a widow, he may be flashing word that he would like to take the widow, but wants Albert's okay. Duncan, the other opponent, passes.

Here, Albert can make a bid of 300, just ten points more than Conrad's. Ordinarily, this would be a meaningless bid, but now Albert uses it to tell his partner to go ahead. So if Barney goes to 310, Conrad can go to 350, the bid he wanted to make. Or, if Barney passes, Conrad can still to go 350, but in that case, he couldn't, if Albert hadn't inserted that ten-point bid. However, if Duncan, instead of passing, had bid 310, Albert could have passed, because the bidding would still be open when it got around to Conrad.

That means that the ten-point cue is a device used by two partners to clarify or solidify their bidding. But it is especially important when bonus scores are injected into the game, to encourage higher bidding. These give bonus points to bidders who win their bids at 300 and upward. They are commonly used in Firehouse Pinochle, but may be introduced to the other forms of Partnership play as well. They are described under the heading of *Bonus Melds*.

down to solid earth, a player who already has a Sequence or Four Aces in hand, with no need for a fill can still count on 40 or 50 points from the four-card widow and can stretch his bid accordingly.

Special Rules with the Widow: Normally, the successful bidder is required to turn the widow face up so that the other players can see what he got and what they didn't get. By agreement beforehand, that rule can be eliminated, letting the successful bidder keep the widow to himself. It is customary for the player to make his four-card discard face down; but here, a rule may be injected that if the bidder puts away a trump, he must show it to the other players. This gives them a fair chance to calculate the odds of a trick being trumped.

Some players feel that a four-card widow is really too big. This has led to an optional rule to this effect: The successful bidder alone looks at the widow, but he is allowed to keep only *one card* which he keeps in his hand. He deals the other three face down to the other players — naturally giving the best choice to his partner — and they also keep them, thus giving everybody a standard twelve-card hand.

Oddly, this seldom curtails a big bidder, because he is usually counting on a single card to bring his hand up to the level of his bid. He may bid more confidently if he has a choice of three instead of only two, but if he gets one, that should be enough. But it restrains the solid bidders who don't have to fill their hands, but are banking on the widow to bring those 40 or 50 points as insurance. Getting a lone card from the widow isn't much help.

In this version, there is no discard, and therefore no cards can be put away. The bidder may find himself stuck with some losing counters. But all things considered, this is a good rule, particularly because it involves play with twelve-card hands. Adoption of the option is therefore recommended.